Economics for Collaborative Environmental Management

For
Lisa, Vincent and Veronica
and Patricia, my mother, 1934–2003

Economics for Collaborative Environmental Management

Renegotiating the Commons

Graham R. Marshall

London • Sterling, VA

First published by Earthscan in the UK and USA in 2005

ISBN: 1-84407-094-8   hardback
        1-84407-095-6   paperback

Typesetting by Fish Books
Printed and bound in the UK by Bath Press, Bath
Cover design by Danny Gillespie

For a full list of publications please contact:

Earthscan
8–12 Camden High Street
London, NW1 0JH, UK
Tel: +44 (0)20 7387 8558
Fax: +44 (0)20 7387 8998
Email: earthinfo@earthscan.co.uk
Web: **www.earthscan.co.uk**

22883 Quicksilver Drive, Sterling, VA 20166-2012, USA

Earthscan publishes in association with WWF-UK and the International Institute
for Environment and Development

A catalogue record for this book is available from the British Library

Library of Congress Cataloging-in-Publication Data has been applied for

This book is printed on elemental chlorine-free paper

Contents

List of Figures and Tables

Figures

Tables

Acknowledgements

As an economist employed by the New South Wales (NSW) Department of Agriculture at Yanco Agricultural Institute, I found myself in the early 1990s involved in collaborative programs of irrigation salinity management that my neoclassical training suggested would inevitably fall prey to pervasive free riding and rent seeking. Even so, enough evidence of benefits from these community-based collaborative experiments accumulated that I started to seek an economic explanation of how these benefits arise. I am indebted to the participants in these programmes, from both the irrigator community and government, for opening my eyes to the potential of collaborative environmental management and the need for economists to understand and help realize this potential. I was fortunate at the time to be part of a statewide team of departmental economists with an inspiring track record of enhancing decision making by governments and farmers through research.

My opportunity to explore how economics might analyze collaborative environmental management more usefully arrived with a move in 1995 to the Department of Agricultural and Resource Economics at the University of New England. Thank you Garry Griffith for encouraging the move. More particularly, the opportunity arose with the offer in 1997 of a scholarship for PhD research into the economics of integrated catchment (watershed) management, which policy makers around Australia introduced in the late 1980s and early 1990s as a collaborative method of developing and implementing integrated solutions to natural resource and environmental problems. My appreciation goes to the Australian Research Council (ARC), which funded the scholarship stipend, and to the then NSW Department of Land and Water Conservation (DLWC), which acted as industry partner to the project and provided generous financial and in-kind support. Ron Cullen and Tony McGlynn from DLWC were each most accessible and insightful as my primary contacts with their agency. Warren Musgrave was instrumental in identifying the research topic and spurring the scholarship application. A special vote of thanks is due for his ongoing encouragement. Gratitude for financial support towards doctoral fieldwork goes also to the River Basin Management Society for an Ernest Jackson Memorial Research Grant, and to the University of New England for a Keith and Dorothy Mackay Postgraduate Travelling Scholarship.

It was my great fortune to have a team of dissertation supervisors – Brian Dollery, Bruce Hooper, Paul Winters, Geoff Harris and Chris Lloyd – supportive of the intellectual freedom required to look afresh at the economics of collaboration in environmental management. My gratitude goes to you for the open minds, diverse perspectives and formidable talents you brought to a many-sided topic.

The hospitality and ideas extended to me by the staff of the Flood Hazard

Research Centre, at London's Middlesex University, during my month with them in late 1997 remains fondly remembered. I am grateful also to Murray Irrigation Limited for the crucial logistical support it provided towards my doctoral fieldwork, and to the irrigators and other stakeholders who participated in the in-depth interviews.

Attending the Biennial Conference of the International Association for the Study of Common Property at Indiana University's Bloomington campus in 2000 was a real highlight of my time as a doctoral student. Meanwhile, the continuing interest in my work from Australian agricultural and resource economists has been most sustaining. The invitations from the Western Australian and NSW branches of the Australian Agricultural and Resource Economics Society (AARES) to make presentations on my research offered me timely encouragement as well as valuable feedback. I was tremendously grateful to be awarded the 2003 AARES prize for best PhD research.

My working life post PhD has been spent most congenially and productively with a marvellous bunch of people known as the Institute for Rural Futures, located at the University of New England. I am beholden to David Brunckhorst and Ian Reeve of the Institute for their efforts in preparing the application to the ARC for funds for a postdoctoral fellowship that allowed me, among much else, to submit book proposals and convert the dissertation into a book – and also of course to the ARC for granting the funds. Thank you also to Brendan Doyle and Elaine Barclay for finding a way for me to free up some time for the book at a time when other commitments threatened to sabotage completion.

A highlight during these postdoctoral years was a study tour in 2003 including week-long visits with Margaret McKean at Duke University, and with Elinor and Vincent Ostrom and their excellent colleagues at Indiana University's Workshop for Political Theory and Policy Analysis. I remain deeply appreciative of the warm hospitality extended to my family during each visit, and for the opportunity at both places to present seminars (sponsored at Duke University jointly by the Center for Environmental Solutions and the Department of Political Science, and at Indiana University by the Center for Institutions, Population and Environmental Change) in order to obtain feedback on my research. A generous contribution towards the costs of the study tour was made by the Ian Potter Foundation.

Aside from the individuals already mentioned, I would like to express my appreciation to the many other people whose advice influenced this book – without implicating them in its remaining limitations. Chapter 1 benefited considerably from constructive criticisms of earlier drafts by Clark Millar and Allan Randall. A meeting with Daniel Bromley in Madison in 2000 led me to consider more carefully how the new institutional economics relates to collaborative environmental management. Ray Challen and Laura McCann also made telling contributions. Questions and feedback from participants at the various seminars I presented were also greatly valued. I would also like to acknowledge here the wonderful start in research that the late Bruce Davidson gave me in supervising my undergraduate honours dissertation at the University of Sydney.

The encouraging and patient support of Earthscan, and particularly Rob West, during preparation of this book has been greatly appreciated. It was a time of emotional upheaval during which my mother died courageously from cancer and our daughter Veronica entered the world.

I would like to record here my immense appreciation for my brother Simon and his family – Loretta, Fabienne and Talitha – moving from London to Sydney for almost two years after mum passed away. It made our world so much brighter. I also cannot let this opportunity pass to thank my father, Trevor, and my sister, Alison, for all the precious times we continue to spend together.

Lisa, I could not have written this book without your amazing love.

Vincent, you are three years old. Veronica, you are not yet one. You are both so beautiful.

List of Acronyms and Abbreviations

CAMPFIRE	Communal Areas Management Programme for Indigenous Resources
CIG	Community Implementation Group
CPR	common pool resource
CWG	community working group
DNPWLM	Department of National Parks and Wildlife Management
DLWC	Department of Land and Water Conservation
DWR	Department of Water Resources
FAO	Food and Agriculture Organization
HoA	Heads of Agreement
IAD	Institutional Analysis and Development
IFRI	International Forestry Resources and Institutions
IMB	Irrigation Management Board
LWMP	Land and Water Management Plan/ning
LWMPAT	Land and Water Management Planning Assessment Team
MDBC	Murray Darling Basin Commission
MDBMC	Murray Darling Basin Ministerial Council
MIL	Murray Irrigation Limited
NIE	new institutional economics
NIA	National Irrigation Administration (the Philippines)
NSW	New South Wales
RAP	remedial action plan
RFA	Regional Forest Agreement
SRIDC	Southern Riverina Irrigation Districts' Council
UNCED	United Nations Conference on Environment and Development
WNIE	Williamson school of the new institutional economics
WSSD	World Summit on Sustainable Development

Introduction

Collaborative environmental management: Vision or hallucination?

A new vision for collective action in environmental and natural resource management arose to worldwide prominence during the 1990s. It was based on a belief that fostering collaboration between the different civil groups and government agencies with an interest in the outcomes of this management ('stakeholders') would lead them to cooperate with one another more voluntarily in implementing the decisions arising from this collaboration. Here it is called the 'collaborative vision'. The impetus for its emergence can be found in growing recognition within both government and civil society that the inherited dominant way of organizing this management, derived from the 'Progressive vision' for collective action, is ill-adapted for coping with the kinds of complex environmental and natural resource problems emerging nowadays with increasing rapidity.

The Progressive vision views the world as the sum of its parts, and presumes consequently that the best solution to any given problem will be found by dividing it into parts, solving the parts separately, and then packaging together the partial answers as an integrated solution. This vision was influenced strongly too by fears regarding the irrationality of the 'public', which in common usage includes everyone except those regarded as experts (Owens, 2000). Hence, it favoured collective action problems being assigned to centralized ('monocentric') organizational systems wherein the problems are solved solely by experts assigned to different parts of the problems, and the activities of the experts are all coordinated by a single integrated command structure.

Collaboration has been defined as '(1) the pooling of appreciations and/or tangible resources..., (2) by two or more stakeholders, (3) to solve a set of problems that neither can solve individually' (Gray, 1985, p912). It relies on voluntary cooperation, which 'involves individuals or groups moving in concert in a situation in which no party has the power to command the behaviour of others' (Wondolleck and Yaffee, 2000, pxiii). Collaborative approaches to collective action can therefore be regarded as 'polycentric' in the sense that they comprise 'many centers of decision making that are formally independent of each other' (Ostrom et al, 1999b, p32).

It is widely accepted nowadays by national governments, in large part due to the influence of sustainable development discourse and particularly *Agenda 21* (United Nations, 1992a) and the *Rio Declaration on Environment and Development* (United Nations, 1992b), that success with collaborative approaches to environmental and natural resource management depends on inclusive participation by the various communities and other publics with interests in the problems being addressed (Pretty and Ward, 2001; Conley and Moote, 2003). Programmes of government–community collaboration in environmental management, wherein significant responsibilities for collective action are decentralized to communities, are indeed coming to be seen as an important way of scaling up and institutionalizing popular participation (Ribot, 2002).

Approaches to environmental and resource management involving collaboration as typified above have been called a range of names, including: collaborative stewardship, public–private partnerships, community-based collaboration, community-based (or community-driven) natural resource management, integrated environmental management, co-management, participatory watershed management, adaptive ecosystem management and civic environmentalism. Some idea of the rate at which adoption of such approaches is increasing is given by the estimate of Mansuri and Rao (2003) that the World Bank's lending for community-driven development projects increased from US$325 million in 1996 to $2 billion in 2003.

The escalating adoption of approaches to environmental and resource management referred to by governments and aid donors as collaborative, community-based and the like has not come without disappointments, and these disappointments have spurred a formidable backlash. For instance, Conley and Moote (2003, p373) have reported that in the US '[m]any environmental groups charge that these [collaborative] efforts are co-opted by local economic development interests while industry groups contend the opposite'. Bryan (2004, p881) found similarly that many environmentalists argue that collaborative approaches 'are an abdication of government authority, circumvent environmental laws, lead to lowest common denominator solutions, are not accountable to public and scientific review processes, and are undemocratic'. Perhaps the most fundamental criticism of such approaches is that few of them have effected changes in on-ground behaviour fast enough given the scale of the problems they face – and particularly that the action strategies developed within such approaches have rarely proceeded to successful implementation (Margerum, 1999).

Proponents of the collaborative vision for environmental management, and for pursuit of sustainable development more generally, argue that it is too early to pass judgement on the merits of this vision until we have learned what it can realistically deliver and how this potential can best be realized. To some extent, the disappointment with collaborative approaches has resulted from unrealistic expectations of what they should be able to achieve. Hence, proponents of collaborative community-based approaches like Conley and Moote (2003, p383) have become 'unnerved by the ways in which these processes have been portrayed as a cure-all'. This excessive optimism often follows from failing to appreciate realistically the obstacles to gaining inclusive community participation in collaborative processes and to governments delivering the effective decentralization of management responsibilities signalled by their collaboration rhetoric (Mandondo, 2000; Agrawal and Gibson, 2001).

Few programmes of environmental and resource management called collaborative or community-based live up to that label, and it is not uncommon that claims of programmes being collaborative are belied in practice by continuing centralization of powers (Mandondo, 2000; Ribot, 2002; deGrassi, 2003). This gap between rhetoric and practice often results from donors making their funding conditional on programme proposals demonstrating commitments to collaboration and community participation, but failing to adequately monitor compliance with those commitments (Child, 2003). The backlash against decentralized, collaborative approaches to environmental and natural resource management is therefore partly a case of mistaken identity. Often it is not collaborative approaches that have failed but rather the people who have promised collaboration while delivering something else in its name (Ribot, 2002; Child and Clayton, 2004. Nevertheless, this mistaken identification of collaborative approaches has inflicted significant damage on its international reputation. Hence, there is a risk that the collaborative vision will be pronounced a hallucination before it has been given a fair chance to prove itself. Ribot (2002, pp18, 19) argued accordingly:

> Before decentralizations can be judged, time is needed for them to be legislated, implemented and take effect.... [To] test the conditions under which it yields the benefits that theorists and advocates promise, decentralization must be fully tested, monitored, and evaluated.

Nevertheless, it would be mistaken to conclude that the backlash against collaborative environmental management is due entirely to its critics focusing predominantly on programmes that fall short of the principles set out for this management by its proponents. It has arisen also because these principles often remain too unsophisticated to be of much use in guiding application of the collaborative approach given its sensitivity to context and its complexity more generally. Hence, some blame for the backlash must be attributed to the proponents of decentralized, collaborative approaches having presented these approaches as simpler than they actually are and underemphasizing the knowledge gaps standing in the way of implementing them with reasonable assurances of success. Andersson (2003, p5) found accordingly that '[t]he scientific understanding of the institutional and environmental effects of decentralization reform remains quite limited in most countries, even where such reforms have been carried out for some time'. Rhoades (2000, pp334, 341) observed along similar lines in respect of international attempts at collaborative watershed management that:

> Failure, if it occurs, will not be caused by the critics, but because the proponents... of this exciting approach have not done their homework... If we do not convene soon to share experiences, learn from our mistakes, and provide hard-hitting assessments of the multipurpose participatory watershed project, the baby may indeed go out with the bathwater. Our hearts may be in the right place, but where are our heads?

Focus and structure of the book

This book aims to help with this homework. In particular, it seeks to provide a foundation of theory and method from which economic analysis can begin to contribute towards the knowledge needed to successfully pursue the collaborative vision for environmental and natural resource management.

This focus is important for two main reasons. First, as discussed in Chapter 1, the worldview of mainstream economics remains closely linked with the Progressive vision. Contemporary mainstream economics is therefore ill-equipped to understand the need in contemporary environmental management to shift from the Progressive vision to a collaborative vision – let alone to make sense of and learn from experiences accumulated in pursuing the collaborative vision. As highlighted in Chapter 2, one way in which mainstream economics is ill-suited to analysing experiences and options in collaborative environmental management is that it predicts voluntary cooperation within a group of any significant size to be impossible as a result of the 'free rider problem' – even if its members have collaborated previously and thereby agreed to cooperate in a certain way. The implication is that the collaborative vision is indeed a hallucination, and consequently that time spent in its pursuit is time wasted. Indeed, most economists remain sceptical of truly collaborative approaches to collective action.

Mainstream economics is also inappropriate for analysing collaborative environmental management because it assumes problems of institutional design can invariably be solved optimally at the outset, no matter how complex these problems are. As discussed in Chapter 4, this remains the case with most adherents of the new institutional economics, an extension of mainstream economics that claims to account for the limits of human cognition in solving problems of institutional choice. In contrast, it is widely accepted among analysts of collaborative environmental management that this management involves such complexity that we can only hope to discover its optimal design for any context by learning gradually from experience – via a scientific process of institutional experimentation known as 'adaptive management' (Bellamy and Johnson, 2000; Wondolleck and Yaffee 2000; Berkes, 2002; Wilson, 2002). Since mainstream economics proceeds as if all institutional choices in respect of collaborative environmental management are made optimally at the outset, it effectively denies any value for the learning opportunities associated with institutional choices that proponents of adaptive management emphasize as important.

Second, mainstream economics remains arguably the social-scientific tradition with greatest influence over how collective action in environmental and natural resource management is organized. As explained in Chapter 1, this position of influence came about in significant measure because mainstream economists played to the hold on the bureaucratic and public imagination of Progressive beliefs about what constitutes good science. It is understandable, therefore, that mainstream economists would be reluctant to contribute towards knowledge that reveals these beliefs to be no longer required; namely, the knowledge needed for successful transition to the collaborative vision.

Even so, the bureaucratic and public imagination is moving on, and mainstream economists need to follow if they are to avoid longer-term irrelevancy. The sooner they choose to follow, rather than use their waning but still powerful influence to uphold the Progressive vision, the sooner will mainstream economics expedite rather than impede the important contribution of the social sciences to bringing the collaborative vision to fruition. However, they cannot follow usefully until they have, first, a theoretical foundation enabling them to comprehend the collaborative vision and the need for its pursuit through adaptive management, and, second, a method that can be used to develop this foundation to a level of sophistication that facilitates credible economic analysis of policy options for realizing this vision.

This book is structured in four parts. Part I consists of Chapter 1, which presents a historical perspective on how the collaborative vision for environmental and natural resource management emerged to challenge the Progressive vision, and why, in many settings, this challenge is yet to make significant headway. The role of mainstream economics in upholding the Progressive vision in the face of this challenge is explored in particular.

Part II offers a foundation of theory and method with which economic analysis can start to grapple with the complexity of realizing the collaborative vision for environmental and natural resource management. It begins in Chapter 2 with a brief review of what mainstream economics concludes about collective action in environmental and natural resource management, particularly in terms of voluntary cooperation helping to avoid the 'tragedy of the commons' (Hardin, 1968). Chapter 3 discusses the weaknesses of this approach to analysing the economics of collective action in managing environmental problems, and presents a review and synthesis of developments in theory designed to correct these weaknesses. Chapter 4 begins by exploring the implications of these developments for the complexity of economic analysis concerned with institutional choices arising in pursuit of the collaborative vision. A key implication is that the capacity of collaborative systems of environmental management to solve complex problems can be expected to grow the more that they are given scope to develop as 'nested' types of polycentric systems – that is, multi-layered systems within which organizational units at any level complement, rather than absorb or sideline, the self-organizing capacities of units 'below' them. The chapter proceeds to develop a cost effectiveness framework that accounts for this complexity and equips economists methodologically to analyse these institutional choices in accordance with the precepts of adaptive management. The challenge of using inductive analysis to apply those specific elements of the framework designed to capture the complexity, and associated path dependency, of institutional choices is highlighted.

Part III presents a range of lessons about successful collaborative environmental management that have been distilled from case studies in this domain. The case study method has been a mainstay of research efforts to learn inductively from experiences in community-based and other collaborative approaches to environmental management. Chapter 5 synthesizes lessons from an international array of case studies reported previously. The focus here is on lessons relevant to organizing community-based collaborative systems of environmental management successfully as nested systems. Chapter 6 presents lessons from a single case study undertaken by the author. The case studied is a leading Australian community-based collaborative programme concerned with irrigation-induced resource degradation problems – initially waterlogging and soil and water salinization – in a part of that country's Murray Darling Basin. The focus here is on exploring how the theoretical developments discussed in Chapter 3, particularly concerned with trust and other elements of social capital, help us to understand and learn from the behaviour of individuals faced with an actual large group problem of collective action.

Part IV considers, on the basis of the material presented earlier, how the capacities of governments, communities and researchers to expedite pursuit of the collaborative vision for environmental management might be strengthened most effectively. Chapter 7 addresses this question in detail. The discussion of how researchers might best contribute includes a research strategy for economists to follow in applying the framework presented earlier for analysing and predicting the cost effectiveness of alternative institutional paths towards the collaborative vision. Chapter 8 closes the book with some thoughts on the deep-seated cultural obstacles to be faced by economists and others in applying themselves in the decades ahead to the task of realizing this vision, and a call for patient but concerted efforts to surmount these obstacles.

This book is concerned equally with pursuit of the collaborative vision in environmental management and natural resource management. To simplify exposition, however, the term 'collaborative environmental management' is often used as shorthand for 'collaborative environmental and natural resource management'.

Part I

The Collaborative Vision:
Hopes and Frustrations

1

Progress, Sustainability and Economics

Why has the collaborative vision for environmental management associated with the sustainable development concept proven difficult to realize? Is the vision naive, based on an overoptimistic view of human nature, or does it – like any prescient vision – outflank what we can comprehend with existing mainstream modes of thinking? After all, it would not be the first time that an important new way of thinking has been rejected persistently for being out of step with established wisdom. Kuhn (1970) highlighted, for instance, how the ideas of Copernicus gained few converts for almost a century after his death, and how Newton's ideas were not widely accepted for more than a half century after their publication.

Many advocates of the sustainable development concept are frustrated at what they see as continuing misinterpretation of what it entails. For example, the Secretary-General of the United Nations lamented that 'while sustainable development may be the new conventional wisdom, many people have still not grasped its meaning' (Annan, 2002a). The aim in this chapter is to explore whether this frustration is warranted and, if it is, uncover how the mainstream wisdom – particularly in economics – is holding us back in comprehending what is needed to successfully pursue the collaborative vision.

The chapter begins by outlining the beliefs of modernism and how these beliefs came to be reflected within industrialized countries in the Progressive vision for environmental and natural resource management. It goes on to consider intellectual critiques of this vision and how mainstream economics stepped in after World War II to bolster its intellectual credibility by making it more market oriented. The spread of the Progressive model for environmental management to industrializing countries is discussed. The chapter turns then to considering how, from the 1960s onwards, environmentalism and other popular forces emerged that challenged the Progressive vision, and how these forces coalesced in the 1980s and 1990s into broad international consensus around the concept of sustainable development – a concept that emphasizes collaborative approaches to solving environmental problems founded on inclusive public participation. The influence of mainstream economics on how the sustainable development concept has come to be (mis)understood in dominant arenas of public discourse – that is, along the lines of the market-oriented Progressive vision championed by mainstream economics – is then considered. Finally, the importance for the international pursuit of sustainable development and the collaborative vision of economists outgrowing their ideological commitment to the Progressive vision is discussed.

Modernism and the Progressive vision

Modernism[1]

The origins of the Western worldview can be traced to Judaism, which taught that the Earth and all life on it were created by a single God according to a grand design (Norgaard, 1994). René Descartes (1596–1650) is credited as originating modern philosophy. His proclamation, translated as 'I think, therefore I am', sought to transfer the authority of Reason from religious and other traditional structures to every individual, thereby preparing the ground for a secular science committed to neutrality with regard to questions of meaning and value. Science thus came to imagine people as similar to God; that is to say, as outside the world over which they had dominion. This premise has been called 'objectivism', a belief that people can remain apart from the system they are seeking to understand and act upon.

The idea of God having created the world according to a grand design persisted within secular science, translated into the belief of 'universalism'. The underlying nature of the myriad phenomena of the world, as well as the relationships between them, was assumed explainable by a relatively small number of simple, and discoverable, universal principles.

In pursuing these universal principles, it came also to be supposed that nature works like a machine. Hence, the relations between the parts of any natural system were assumed constant, and the system was believed to have a unique equilibrium configuration for any given combination of conditions. Any natural system was expected accordingly to exhibit regular behaviour, enabling prediction of how it would respond to changes in its conditions. These assumptions have been characterized as the belief of 'mechanism'.

Along with mechanism was the associated belief – known as 'atomism' – that natural systems consist of unchanging parts, and are simply the sum of their parts. It follows that the parts are knowable independently, and that any problem with a natural system can be solved by breaking the problem into parts, investigating each part separately, and then simply combining the parcels of knowledge thus obtained.

A further key belief entering Western science was 'monism' – that there is a single best way of understanding any given natural system. If more than one way of understanding does exist at any time, this belief implies that science will eventually reveal that these ways of understanding fit together into one coherent understanding.

The monumental advances in knowledge that Isaac Newton (1643–1727) and others obtained from applying these five key 'modernist' beliefs – objectivism, universalism, mechanism, atomism and monism – to investigating the natural world during the scientific revolution, and that James Watt (1736–1819) and others achieved technologically during the subsequent industrial revolution, imbued these beliefs with an aura of objectivity. When the social sciences began to coalesce in the mid-18th century, therefore, it was against a background of these five metaphysical and epistemological beliefs having contributed so successfully to understanding the natural world. In consequence, the 'principle of unity of the scientific method' arose within the social sciences, proclaiming that the premises of natural science are directly transferable to the social world (Wacquant, 1993). As objectivism became translated into beliefs about the use of science in understanding and managing social systems, it became referred to frequently as 'positivism'. Positivism came to dominate the philosophy of science until critiques from 'post-positivists' emerged from the 1960s onwards.

The five core beliefs underpinning the scientific revolution thus made strong inroads to the social sciences, or at least to those of its disciplines amenable to positivism. Positivists were convinced that social science, like natural science, could be used instrumentally to enhance human welfare: predicting the consequences of alternative options for action and thereby facilitating rational choice between the options in line with the values of the relevant public. The constellation of beliefs surrounding positivism thus reduced life to a gigantic machine that would be eventually be subject to man's control', with history expected to unfold through 'a ceaseless advance of technology as scientists steadily cracked God's grand design' (Norgaard, 1994, p182).

The Progressive Conservation Movement

Indeed, the beliefs underlying positivism were so productive for science in explaining, and yielding technologies to control, natural phenomena that people throughout Western societies were, by the 19th century, taking progress for granted. Over the last two decades of that century and the first two of the 20th century, public confidence in science and progress attained heights never matched since (Nelson, 1987). Even so, a 'Progressive' movement emerged in the US during this time, its members frustrated with what they saw as a wasteful lack of direction in realizing their country's potential for progress. In place of what was then a loosely organized and decentralized society, members of this movement ('Progressives') urged 'development' – a conscious process of making progress happen. They saw the prevailing faith in automatic evolution to a better society as responsible for unproductive economic rivalry, and for spawning a proliferation of civil groups with parochial interests at odds with gaining undivided loyalty to the idea of national development (Hays, 1959).

Inspired by the management techniques based on administrative science that were revolutionizing American capitalism at the time, Progressives argued that government programs could, and should, also be administered scientifically. They shared also a faith in the unambiguous givenness of public problems and values (Croly, 1909).

Accordingly, their emphasis was on efficient means rather than on the ends of collective action. They argued further that government functions could and should be divided into two distinct types. The realm of 'politics' would be confined to addressing basic questions regarding values and policy direction. The distinct realm of 'administration' would regard these values and directions as externally determined, and thus objective, and pursue them efficiently.

Aside from a foundation in objectivism, the Progressive vision for collective action was also founded firmly in the other four modernist beliefs identified above. It was universalist in its confidence that phenomena widely dispersed in space and time could be understood by applying a few basic principles, and that solutions to local problems could therefore be devised from afar by a single, central authority. Progressives' faith in their capacity to predict the consequences of alternative decision options, in order to choose rationally between them and plan comprehensively the implementation of the option chosen (hence 'rational-comprehensive planning'), was grounded in mechanism. Atomism justified their faith that accurate analysis of any given administrative problem could proceed by dividing it into parts, assigning the parts to separate administrative agencies with distinct kinds of expertise, and deriving the whole solution as the sum of the partial answers thus obtained. It also was responsible for Progressives adopting an individualistic conception of democracy, characterized by Hays (1959, p269) as 'social atomism'. This stance stemmed from a fear that democracy as a collaborative and deliberative process would result in individuals' values and preferences evolving against the subjective knowledge of their local groupings rather than against the expanding body of objective knowledge upon which the Progressive vision was founded.

Monism was also central to Progressive thinking, in at least two ways. First, it justified their faith that the diverse subjective knowledge held by individuals would steadily converge on objective scientific knowledge. Since Progressives also believed that scientific consensus would come to extend across ever wider areas of social concern, this faith meant they expected fewer and fewer social choices would need to be based on subjective considerations, including ethical and other 'non-scientific' value systems, they saw as retarding progress (Nelson, 1987). Second, monism justified a faith that the answers found by different agencies and disciplines to the parts of a problem assigned to them would all ultimately fit within a single coherent way of understanding the problem (Norgaard, 1994).

As children of the industrial revolution, Progressives came to regard materialistic values as the relevant 'scientific' yardstick of human progress. Their idea of the public interest centred primarily on increasing industrial output, with other goals emphasized only when their pursuit would help achieve their primary goal (Hays, 1959). Claims to objectivity could also be defended more easily in relation to material phenomena, since typically they are quantified more easily and thus turned into 'facts' (Nelson, 1987).

The conservation professions in the US were at the forefront of championing and applying Progressive ideas, coalescing during the 1890s to 1920s into what became known as the Progressive Conservation Movement. Members of this movement were alarmed at the uncontrolled overexploitation of natural resources that had arisen in the second half of the 1800s and convinced that '[t]echnical experts divorced from the corrupting influences of the politics of the times could best determine the public's interest' (Wondolleck and Yaffee, 2000, p11). The movement brought about important changes that were necessary at the time. Although Progressive Conservationists recognized the existence of physical limits to increasing industrial productivity, and admitted some fears that continuing exploitation of natural resources would eventually create critical scarcities, they were optimistic that science and technology could push back these limits by alleviating waste and inefficiency in resource use. Hence, they were devoted materialists, unsympathetic to the views of other conservationists that certain natural resources (e.g. wilderness areas) should be protected from industrial use for aesthetic or other non-materialistic reasons (Hays, 1959).

By the end of the 19th century, the Progressive vision for collective action had become well established in many Western industrialized countries. Due to the rapid productivity gains and improvements in material living conditions in these countries during the late 19th and early 20th centuries, their populations became 'thoroughly enamored' of science to the extent that '[i]t was quite natural that the metaphysical and epistemological beliefs widely held at the time by scientists and the public became tightly embedded in our public institutions' (Norgaard, 1994, p69).

Critiques of the Progressive vision

World War I was the first of a succession of events during the 20th century that raised fundamental doubts about the inevitability of human progress. Despite the faith of Progressives that human conflict would fade away as ideological, religious and other 'divisive' ways of thinking converged steadily upon scientific rationality, the human cost of war, terrorism and other forms of conflict seemed to be escalating (Nelson, 1987, p762).

The Progressive vision for collective action also experienced a loss of faith, at least among intellectuals. It was found rarely to be the case in practice that basic social values and policy directions are set clearly in the political realm before being turned over to the administrative realm (Appleby, 1949). Social values were found to be discovered only incrementally as a result of ongoing interaction between and within legislative, judicial and administrative bodies (Lindblom, 1965). Indeed, public problems themselves turned out to be much more ambiguous than Progressives had supposed. It was found that such problems often become defined only through the process of trying to discover acceptable solutions.

In addition, the discipline of administrative science expected to underpin Progressive public administration was revealed by Herbert Simon (1946) to lack a scientific basis, its principles often contradictory platitudes. Faith in administrative rationality as capable of identifying the best option for pursuing a given direction and planning comprehensively its implementation was undermined further by arguments that human rationality in all but exceptional cases is 'bounded' and capable of only satisfactory performance in such tasks (March and Simon, 1958). Also, many of the most innovative developments in scientific thought – for instance, those associated with evolutionary theory, quantum mechanics and game theory – were not founded exclusively on the modernist beliefs underpinning the Progressive vision.

Progressive beliefs had nevertheless become so deeply embedded in the culture of politics and administration and in the public imagination that to question them publicly was tantamount to forfeiting one's right to be taken seriously within this culture or within public discourse. Moreover, the faith in progress justified by these beliefs served to reduce political conflict by making competing interests more likely to compromise now in the expectation that new opportunities would emerge later. Those with power to protect thus had good reason to exploit their privileged positions in public discourse to bolster faith in the Progressive model and its underlying beliefs. This meant that intellectual challenges to these beliefs tended to be reinterpreted with their incorporation to public discourse. Charles Darwin's theory of evolution became popularized, for instance, as vindicating faith in progress as well as ongoing inequalities in power and wealth (Norgaard, 1994).

Another reason for the continuing hold of Progressive ideas on public discourse after the disillusionment of World War I was the emergence of a need in Western democracies to demonstrate that democracy could be effective in the face of the challenges of communism and fascism. Until the mid-1960s or so, this need served to legitimize the depoliticization of many areas of public policy, acceptance of the authority of technical standards in choosing and implementing such policy, and centralized administration (Ezrahi, 1990).

The Progressive vision and economics

In particular, Keynesian economics showed how moderate social engineering by the state could be rationalized as consistent with liberal individualism. Keynesianism provided an opening after World War II for economists to fill the intellectual void that had arisen with accumulating criticism of Progressive ideas as originally laid out. They could agree that the aspiration of achieving all public goals through direct administration – and rational-comprehensive planning in particular – was unrealistic and unworkable, and at the same time offer as a substitute the idea that these goals be attained by the state intervening in the market on the basis of economic advice. The Progressive dichotomy advocated by economists thus came to involve political definition of objectives leading into expert realization of those objectives via state manipulation of the 'market mechanism'. Where direct administration could not be avoided, because market manipulation was impractical or politically unacceptable, economists advocated the alternative of making economic analysis a central element of administrative decision making (Nelson, 1987).

To be sure, this latter role for economic analysis had already become important during the inter-war years, at least in the US where cost–benefit analyses were originally performed by government agencies – and typically by engineers – and usually accepted by the public solely on the basis of agency authority. This authority came under attack around 1940, however, with the findings of cost–benefit analyses challenged by powerful commercial interests. Agencies with competing charters also began to challenge each other's analyses. Pressures arose consequently to objectify the procedures of cost–benefit analysis in the hope of removing suspicions of incompetence or bias in its application. By the 1950s, this was becoming increasingly difficult with agencies expected to account for more and more benefits that could not be so easily quantified. The new welfare economics came to the rescue with its presumption that all human pleasures and pains are commensurable under a single, coherent and quantifiable utility function. In this way, intellectual justification was provided for attempting to value in monetary terms matters like recreation, health and loss of life that had previously been regarded as intangible. By the late 1950s, cost–benefit analysis had become a respectable specialization within economics and it became accepted that the solution to bias or incompetence in this area was to appoint economists to do the job (Porter, 1995).

The roots of the new welfare economics lay in the ordinalist revolution that occurred within neoclassical economics in the 1930s. The concerns of the earlier marginalist school of neoclassical economics had included poverty alleviation and income redistribution. Members of this school contended that utility is observable and comparable across individuals, and accordingly that it is possible to maximize social welfare by maximizing the sum of utilities across individuals. Ordinalists refuted this possibility and, in turn, the possibility of the distributional questions of interest to the marginalists ever being resolved objectively (Batie, 1989). Their solution was to provide a technical fix to such questions and move on promptly to tractable issues conducive to the objectivity and consensus needed for economics to be regarded as scientific by governments and the public.

This technical fix was based on 'Pareto efficiency', a situation where it is not possible to make any individual better off without simultaneously making at least one other individual worse off. This standard of distributional equity justifies a change to the status quo only when the change represents a 'Pareto improvement' – that is, it makes at least one person better off without making anyone worse off. Since this hurdle proved to be too onerous in the real world where virtually all policy options make at least a few individuals worse off, it was soon replaced by the 'potential Pareto improvement' criterion. According to this criterion, a proposed change should be approved if it makes some people better off, even if it makes others worse off, provided that the gainers could compensate the losers and still be better off than they were before the change. This criterion relies on a number of value judgements, including a presumption that the marginal utility of any given money unit (e.g. dollar) is identical across all individuals irrespective of how rich or poor they might be. This means that the incidence of benefits and costs of a change is taken as irrelevant to its effect on collective welfare (Bromley, 1989). As controversial as this value judgement might be, it allowed economists to side-step complicated philosophical and political disputes and substitute precise calculation for judgement (Ezrahi, 1990).

The quest for objectivity also led mainstream economists to seek 'theory of a kind which can only work with stable subject-matter. They need economic behaviour to have a motive force as simple and unchangeable as the gravitational force on which Newtonian physics relies' (Stretton and Orchard, 1994, p19). This need was satisfied through adopting individualism, with aggregate economic behaviour assumed to be the outcome of each individual acting in accordance with his or her ranking of preferences ('self-interest'). The need for this assumption was emphasized by Kenneth Arrow's (1951) Impossibility Theorem which indicated that a stable, unique preference ranking for a group cannot be derived from the preference rankings of its members without retreating from classical liberalism's commitment to protecting individuals' rights of privacy (Ezrahi, 1990; Ball and Dagger, 1995). This commitment entered economics as the principle of consumer (or individual) sovereignty; that is, of democracy requiring that individuals form their preferences independently and, consequently, of economists accepting these preferences as 'sovereign' or given (Norton et al, 1998). Without the prospect of deriving unique preference rankings, economists would have been precluded from identifying a single solution for each public problem and thus from maintaining the apparent objectivity of precision needed to satisfy their Progressive aspirations (Nelson, 1987; Norgaard, 1994).

The economics profession was indeed successful in capitalizing on the intellectual void arising from criticisms of the original Progressive model. Economics in the postwar years came to provide arguably the most important intellectual justification for centralized government in liberal-democratic politics (Nelson, 1987; Ezrahi, 1990). While most economists tended to view their proper professional role as that of neutral experts divorced from politics and subjective judgements, those with practical experience in government soon realized the naivety of this view (Nelson, 1987). Buchanan and Tulloch (1962) laid intellectual foundations that led to various economic theories of government – including the influential theories of public choice and rent-seeking – that assumed all participants in public processes, such as voters, politicians, special interest groups, bureaucrats, experts and even scientists are motivated by their individual self-interest. In these theories, government professionals and the experts and scientists they rely on – the heroes of the Progressive vision – are just self-interested groups like any others. It follows that government agencies frequently become 'captured' by limited constituencies and thus fall short of the Progressive ideal of protecting the much more diffuse, and consequently politically weaker, public interest. This reasoning led to a tendency for government economists to become spokespeople for the public interest in order to balance pressures coming from sectional interests – with the potential Pareto improvement criterion serving as their yardstick of the public interest (Nelson, 1987).

Meanwhile, the second half of the 20th century witnessed the spread of Progressive beliefs and institutions from the West to countries where industrialization had yet to gain widespread momentum. There are a number of reasons for this spread. Industrialization had yielded Western countries considerable wealth and power with which they could impose 'modernization' along Progressive lines upon other countries. At the same time, the elites of these other countries were often keen to modernize so that they might attain similar levels of wealth and power. The West's part in this modernization process was often well-intentioned. Its fervent belief in progress meant that assisting non-Western peoples to jettison their 'backwardness' could be viewed as virtuous even when the help was not wanted (Norgaard, 1994). However, the West's involvement has been self-interested too. For instance, Bromley and Bustelo (1982) observed how analytical techniques associated with Progressive administration, such as cost–benefit analysis, were often prescribed for use in Latin America because international development banks and powerful international consultancy firms stipulated and supported them, enabling these organizations and other firms to profit by selling their knowledge of these techniques.

A vision under siege

Environmentalism

The 1960s were a time of unprecedented affluence for Western countries, and their publics became less concerned with materialistic values associated with natural resources and the environment and more with their aesthetic and amenity values. For a rapidly increasing number of people, these non-materialistic values seemed to be disappearing at a rate threatening the underpinnings of civilized human life they had mostly taken for granted. Thus 'an environmental tsunami slowly built up into the modern environmental movement' (Neimark and Mott, 1999, p180). Nelson (1987, p57) characterized environmentalism as 'a reaction against the core progressive assumptions, particularly the faith that science and technological advance would actually yield much gain to the human spirit'.

In his influential book *Small is Beautiful*, E. F. Schumacher (1973, pp275, 276) voiced as follows the thoughts of many environmentalists:

> In the excitement over the unfolding of his scientific and technical powers, modern man has built a system of production that ravishes nature and a type of society that mutilates man... The development of production and the acquisition of wealth have... become the highest goals of the modern world in relation to which all other goals, no matter how much lip-service may still be paid to them, have come to take second place... This is the philosophy of materialism, and it is this philosophy – or metaphysic – which is being challenged by events... [This challenge] speaks to us in the language of terrorism, genocide, breakdown, pollution, exhaustion.

Environmentalism became an international political issue when the United Nations Conference on the Human Environment brought together representatives from 113 nations in Stockholm in 1972. The natural environment was identified there as critical to successful development, and not merely an obstacle to progress (now defined largely in terms of economic growth) that science and technology would continue steadily to erode.

In the same year of the Stockholm Conference, publication of the Club of Rome's *Limits to Growth* (Meadows et al, 1972) provided influential scientific backing for environmentalist concerns that continuing economic growth was unsustainable given the finiteness of the Earth's capacities to provide material inputs for industrial production and to assimilate the waste outputs from that production. With these arguments adding to the doubts about the inevitability of human progress, mainstream economists again played a prominent role in bolstering faith in progress. Taking their lead from Barnett and Morse (1963), they taught that the only limits to growth are those of human adaptability and inventiveness.

Popular doubts about the inevitability of progress

While economic arguments of this nature offered sufficient intellectual reassurance for Progressive ideas to retain a pervasive influence within the governing process and public discourse, they could not stem the erosion of faith in progress occurring within the general populace of the West. Once the hero of the industrial revolution, the 'machine' had by virtue of an accumulation of wars and other tragedies (e.g. the Bhopal incident and failing nuclear reactors at Chernobyl) turned into a metaphor for war, ecological destruction and the depersonalization of social interaction (Ezrahi, 1990).

Moreover, the Progressive model was leading Western governments into a political and bureaucratic quagmire. From the mid-19th century, the West had been able to increase its living standards dramatically while apparently remaining free of natural limits. As we now know, this freedom was temporary. It arose from the West's access to finite stocks of fossil hydrocarbons – allowing the complexities of capturing solar energy through interacting with ecosystems to be avoided – and the long lags between their use and the cumulative consequences of that use.

By the 1960s, however, natural capacities to assimilate these accumulated consequences were finally becoming overloaded, and a wide range of latent environmental problems and associated social conflicts began rising into view. Meanwhile, the hold of Progressive beliefs upon values celebrated in public life meant that the social identity and status of most Western individuals had come to depend mainly on their own progress in materialistic terms – notwithstanding the recent beginnings of a trend back towards non-materialistic values – and much less on their performance against traditional ethical values. Together with the explosion of materialistic delights spawned by modernization, this shift in the source of individuals' social identity made them ever more reluctant to sacrifice material wealth by paying the taxes needed to address their collective problems. In consequence, the accelerating emergence of environmental problems was far from matched by an upsurge in the fiscal capacities of governments to solve these problems centrally (Norgaard, 1994).

Due to the combination of such factors, the widespread euphoria of mechanistic prediction and control and of overcoming limits to progress started giving way to despondency. Along with despondency came increasingly well informed scepticism of the Progressive project. History may come to regard the most significant consequence of the advance of science up to that time as that of having 'taught different interests how to ask many far more difficult questions' (ibid, p4). By and large, these questions were not arising from an ignorance that could be corrected by sharing greater scientific knowledge with the public, as the monism of Progressives would lead them to conclude (Ezrahi, 1990). Rather, the questions tended to be motivated more by diminishing trust in the epistemological foundations of that knowledge. Owens (2000, p1142) offered this succinct explanation: 'Lay people may not understand the complexities of science... but they are aware of the commercial imperatives, sceptical about politics, and distrustful of the competence and impartiality of regulatory frameworks'.

The historic significance of this change in the public's attitude to the Progressive project was highlighted by Beck (1992, p10, original emphasis) as follows:

> In the nineteenth century, privileges of rank and religious world views were being demystified; today the same is happening to the understanding of science and technology in the classical industrial society. Modernization within the paths of industrial society is being replaced by a modernization of the principles of industrial society... [This emerging new, 'reflexive'] modernity means not less but more modernity, a modernity radicalized against the architecture – e.g. the understanding of 'science', 'progress', 'democracy' – of the classical industrial setting.

Science as a result has become increasingly forced to share with the wider populace the power to define problems, as well as to search for and decide upon solutions to them (Ezrahi, 1990).

International commitment to sustainable development

This historic shift in attitudes towards the Progressive vision was perhaps to become acknowledged most influentially in *Our Common Future*, the Report of the World Commission on Environment and Development (1987). The Report expressed concern that rates of change in society and the natural environment were running ahead of the capacities of scientific disciplines to assess and advise upon, and of existing decision making structures and institutional arrangements to cope with. Of even greater significance was the legitimacy it provided to the widening doubts about each generation inevitably being better off than those preceding it. Indeed, its overall recommendation that human activities be redirected towards 'sustainable development', as defined below, acknowledged the real possibility of negative progress with future generations becoming worse off than the current generation:

> Humanity has the ability to make development sustainable – to ensure that it meets the needs of the present without compromising the ability of future generations to meet their own needs (World Commission on Environment and Development, 1987, p8).

Specific measures for implementing this concept were proposed in the Report which, together with the impetus provided by the *World Conservation Strategy* launched in 1980 (International Union for the Conservation of Nature, 1980), led the United Nations General Assembly to convene the United Nations Conference on Environment and Development (UNCED) in Rio de Janeiro in 1992. The UNCED, or 'Earth Summit', was attended by representatives from 176 governments, including 100 heads of state, as well as from the civil and economic spheres. The Conference elaborated the operational significance of the sustainable development concept through a range of agreements including *Agenda 21* (United Nations, 1992a) as underpinned by the 27 principles contained in the *Rio Declaration on Environment and Development* (United Nations, 1992b).

Economics and sustainable development

Environmental and resource economics

Economists were quick to respond to the challenge that the sustainable development concept presented to the Progressive model, or at least to its acknowledgement that the welfare of future generations could no longer be taken for granted (e.g. Barbier, 1987; Pearce et al, 1989). The foundations for this response had been laid in the recently emerged specializations of environmental economics and natural resource economics. These were subdisciplines of mainstream neoclassical economics and, as such, they were firmly grounded in the updated version of the Progressive vision which, as discussed above, involves political definition of objectives followed by expert manipulation of the market mechanism in order to realize those objectives.

For economists in these subdisciplines, environmental and resource policy problems arise from design flaws in the market mechanism ('market failures') for which remedies exist. Consistent with the Progressive vision, they assume that these flaws and remedies are identifiable through centralized rational analysis, the consequences of the remedies are predictable, and that centralized governments are capable of implementing these remedies.

The type of market failure conventionally of most concern to environmental and resource economists has been that associated with 'externalities' in the provision and appropriation of environmental goods and natural resources. Externalities arise when one party's actions have consequences (positive or negative) for others that are not accounted for in market transactions (Bromley, 1989). A landholder polluting a stream without compensating downstream water users for the damages they incur as a result is one example of a negative externality. Environmental and resource economists interpreted the sustainable development concept as concerned with a particular class of negative externalities; namely, those visited by current generations upon future generations.

The willingness of some prominent environmental and resource economists to engage with the challenge of applying the sustainable development concept represented the beginnings of a retreat within mainstream economics from a faith that economic growth as conventionally (i.e. materialistically) defined would inevitably continue to deliver progress. By this time, environmental and resource economists had also come to acknowledge the significance for human welfare of a wide range of non-materialistic values associated with the natural environment, and the need to include these values in cost–benefit analysis wherever possible by imputing market prices for them through 'non-market valuation' techniques like contingent valuation, hedonic pricing and choice modelling. These accommodations of some key concerns of sustainable development advocates within a mechanistic system of logic allowed environmental and resource economists to continue operating within what essentially remained a Progressive framework, and thus to continue satisfying governmental and public expectations of a scientific profession despite having made significant concessions to environmentalists. This positioning delivered such economists formidable influence in early policy deliberations about the practical policy implications of the sustainable development concept. The title of one of the earliest, and perhaps most influential, environmental economics treatises on this topic – *Blueprint for a Green Economy* (Pearce et al, 1989), the release of which excited newspaper headlines – indicates the confidence with which this influence was exercised.

Nevertheless, the ability of economists working in this field to contribute to practical policy formulation consistently with their Progressive ambitions depended on them agreeing on a rigorous technical definition of sustainable development that would enable precise identification of an optimal solution to any given 'sustainability' problem and thus establish a basis for asserting objectivity. Even with economists limiting their consideration of sustainability to issues of inter-generational equity and finiteness of natural resources (with many more issues identified in Agenda 21 and the Rio Declaration), however, there remains 'no clear understanding of, let alone consensus around, what constitutes a sustainability objective or standard... [W]hat it is, who decides what it is, and how that decision is made, continue to bedevil analysts of all stripes' (Pezzey and Toman, 2002, pxxvii).

Without an objective basis for advising on issues of sustainability as defined through international consensus, environmental and resource economists working in the policy arena tended to interpret sustainability in a way such that they could assert an objective basis of advice does exist; namely, as market failure issues of concern for current generations. The main emphasis in this strategy has been on remedying the market mechanism's failure to account for environmental externalities – the rationale being that this failure amounts to the natural environment being treated in effect as a free good and thus over-used. Two types of remedy have been pursued along these lines. The first involves creating markets for the environmental goods and services associated with the externalities (typically by centralized decision makers establishing an overall limit on the use of an environmental good or service and apportioning the limited overall use among individual users in the form of marketable permits). The second entails modifying existing markets by centrally estimating the value of the externalities (i.e. through non-market valuation methods) and ensuring that these values are incorporated (through 'market-based incentive systems') into the prices of the goods and services whose provision were generating the externalities (Pearce et al, 1989).

The argument of environmental and resource economists – that pressures on the natural environment would be reduced by ensuring that the full costs of its use are accounted for – appealed to many environmentalists who had identified the market's frequent blindness to the environment as an important reason for its degradation (even if economists were concerned only with costs imposed on current generations). The idea of 'making the market work for sustainable development' (United Nations Environment Programme, 2002, p407) thus found its way into international agreements elaborating the significance of the sustainable development concept for practical policy formulation, including in clause 8.29 of Agenda 21: 'Within a supportive international and national economic context and given the necessary legal and regulatory framework, economic and market-oriented approaches can in many cases enhance capacity to deal with issues of environment and development' (United Nations, 1992a).

Limitations of the response from environmental and resource economics

Even so, it is clear from Agenda 21 and the Rio Declaration that market-oriented approaches were regarded by the nations endorsing those documents as just one of the reforms required for transition onto a path of sustainable development. It is clear from those documents, moreover, that market-oriented approaches were intended to be implemented in accordance with a range of values not all supportive of the Progressive framework of environmental economics. For instance, the so-called 'Principle of Common but Differentiated Responsibilities' endorsed in the Rio Declaration (as Principle 7) was recently reiterated by the Secretary-General of the United Nations in the following terms: 'The richest countries must lead the way. They have the wealth. They have the technology. And they contribute disproportionately to global environmental problems' (United Nations, 2002). This insistence that the actual distribution across rich and poor countries of the benefits and costs of moving towards sustainable development does matter is at odds with the criterion of potential Pareto improvement conventionally applied by environmental and resource economists.

A further important way that the concept of sustainable development elaborated in Agenda 21 challenges the Progressive framework of environmental and resource economics – in this case the principle of individual sovereignty – lies in its endorsement of collective efforts (e.g. education, awareness-raising programmes, information provision and advertising) to change individuals' beliefs and values to ones more conducive to their adoption of consumption and production patterns placing less pressure on the natural environment.

Another way lies in its rejection of the Progressive presumption that identification and resolution of all collective problems should be the exclusive domain of centralized governing processes involving only politicians and professional administrators (and their scientific and technical advisors). This rejection is apparent in a number of the Rio Declaration principles, most directly in Principle 10 – 'Environmental issues are best handled with the participation of all concerned citizens, at the relevant level' (United Nations, 1992b). The principle of citizen participation in environmental policy extends to market-oriented policy approaches, justifying arguments that markets for environmental goods and services be shaped by partnerships between government, industry and other community interests (United Nations Environment Programme, 2002).

The final way to be mentioned here of how the sustainable development concept elaborated at the UNCED challenges the Progressive framework of environmental and resource economics lies in its endorsement (in Principle 15 of the Rio Declaration) of a 'precautionary approach' to decisions with possibly irreversible environmental consequences. This approach follows from an acknowledgement in Agenda 21 that 'the future is uncertain, and there will be surprises' and that good policy for the environment and development should therefore 'keep open a range of options to ensure flexibility of response' (United Nations, 1992a, clause 35.5). The precautionary approach has foundations in concepts inherent in the 'science of surprise' that have become incorporated increasingly into ecological science and environmentalism. The principles associated with this 'science of surprise' emphasize 'the impossibility of prediction and the irrelevancy of probabilistic approaches to uncertainty management' (Batie, 1989, p1094). These principles, and thus the precautionary approach, contradict the mechanistic premises of mainstream economics.

Sandra Batie (1989, p1097) is one prominent resource economist who has questioned the wisdom of her colleagues using discredited Progressive beliefs (albeit still widely accepted within environmental and resource economics) about the proper role of science in the governing process to justify sidelining issues raised by the sustainable development concept that they could not address without stepping outside that role. In her Presidential Address to the American Agricultural Economics Association, she observed that the increasing legitimacy of the concept was creating challenges for economists that they could ignore only 'at the peril of increasing irrelevancy' (ibid, p1084). She proceeded to argue, on the grounds that 'policy economics should not be independent of the political expression of society' (ibid, p1097), that policy economists must therefore be concerned with the implications for their analyses of the concept and its underlying premises.

This view echoes Daniel Bromley's (1989, p233, original emphasis) argument, along the following lines, that the notion of objectivity applied in mainstream economics misunderstands what objectivity actually entails: 'It is *not* the science – nor the conclusions – that are objective but rather the economist who stands between theory and the individual(s) who must make a decision with economic content and implications'. In this view, objectivity requires that independent economists reach similar conclusions with respect to how a collectivity can best achieve values and goals it has chosen for itself. Accordingly, he advocated replacing the 'Paretian approach' to economic analysis by a 'decision-making approach' based on a value judgement that it is not an economist's place to question a collectively agreed value system, especially where the process of reaching agreement has been demonstrably democratic. The role of a policy economist following this approach is, therefore, to assist a collectivity make choices consistent with values and objectives it has decided upon democratically for itself. This approach has also been called the 'political economy approach' (Schmid, 1989).

The hold of market fundamentalism

To date, such calls for reorientation within mainstream economics have had little noticeable effect. Since the 1980s, the influence on public policy making of the ideas of political elites has grown markedly. With ideological debate assuming a stronger role in policy making, economists increasingly found themselves defending economic ideas against ideological challenges. The confidence with which they did so and continued to recommend centrally-planned and -implemented market-oriented solutions to public problems was ideologically driven. Although most economists would repudiate such a slur on their objectivity, Nelson (1987, p58) observed that:

> ... any basic way of thinking about social issues rests on fundamental assumptions and values that involve some elements of faith. Economists have such a way of thinking and in this sense they can be said also to have an ideology. While the profession is not monolithic,... the outlook of the mainstream of the profession is still very much influenced by Progressive thinking.

Economic policy advisers thus tended to become propagandists of the values underpinning mainstream economics. They were advantaged in this contest by being able to play to the continuing hold of Progressive ideas on politics, administration and the popular imagination. However, as Kuhn (1970, pp167, 168) found from an historical study of scientific revolutions, science can be depended on to advance knowledge only when appeals for the superiority of competing scientific explanations are made not 'to heads of state or the populace at large' but rather to 'a special kind of community' the members of which know enough to evaluate competently where superiority lies. To the extent that mainstream economists became less discriminating than this in seeking support for their ideas, they became more likely to retard the advance of knowledge than promote it (Norgaard, 1994).

Certainly, despite the commitments made by so many national governments at the Rio Earth Summit, the ideology of sustainable development has yet to make appreciable headway in contesting the pervasive public policy influence of mainstream economics. As the Secretary-General of the United Nations observed recently: 'At discussions on global finance and the economy, the environment is still treated as an unwelcome guest' (Annan, 2002b). He commented elsewhere on how, as a result, 'sustainability... has become a pious invocation, rather than the urgent call to action it should be' (Annan, 2002a).

Globalization has changed the international policy landscape greatly since the Rio Earth Summit. Despite the potential that globalization offers to crystallize the common interests of all humans in learning how to cooperate across national borders in addressing the shared threats of global warming, terrorism, etc., it has been driven increasingly instead by trade and financial liberalization as legitimized by mainstream economic arguments that restrictions on the universality of the market mechanism be lifted. In these circumstances, the loss of momentum in fulfilling humanity's collective aspiration for sustainable development is not unexpected given that markets 'empower people to reach the goals they can reach as individuals but disempower them in their efforts to reach goals that require collective action' (Norgaard, 1994, p153).

As globalization via the path of trade and financial liberalization has proceeded, and the economic progress of nations (as conventionally measured in terms of Gross Domestic Product) has thus become increasingly exposed to how international markets react to their policy choices, pursuit of policy directions at odds with mainstream economic logic – such as sustainable development – has indeed come to put that kind of progress ever more at risk. The scope for national governments to implement the sustainable development concept therefore seems likely to continue diminishing, therefore, until we – in the words of the President of the World Summit on Sustainable Development (WSSD) (and President of South Africa) (United Nations, 2002, Annex II) – 'outgrow market fundamentalism' and learn to revision progress in accordance with this concept.

Bringing economics on board

Advocates of the sustainable development concept are justified in feeling frustrated with how the concept has come to be interpreted conventionally. This interpretation remains grounded in what Beck (1992, p11) has called 'the myth of industrial society'. This myth asserts that a society founded upon the modernist beliefs integral to the scientific and industrial revolutions 'is a *thoroughly modern* society, a pinnacle of modernity, which it scarcely makes sense even to consider surpassing' (ibid, original emphasis, p11). Such is the hold of this myth on public discourse that it has been possible to present the dramatic escalation of environmental and other problems from the second half of the 20th century onwards as evidence of tardiness in completing the modern agenda. The challenge that advocacy of the sustainable development concept presents to modern beliefs thus came to be misinterpreted widely as a call to extend and intensify the application of those beliefs. Connor and Dovers (2004, p227) observed accordingly that national responses so far to the international call for sustainable development 'suggest a common assumption that just doing things a bit differently, through marginal change mostly within the environmental policy domain, will be sufficient'.

We have seen in this chapter how mainstream economics, particularly its subdiscipline of environmental and resource economics, contributed to this misinterpretation. Our failures in pursuit of sustainable development stem not only from market failures, as this economics suggests, but also crucially from failures to adapt the beliefs, values and insitutions that continue to propel us along unsustainable trajectories. Much of the remainder of this book is concerned with exploring how economics can make a more enlightened contribution towards translating the sustainable development concept – as re-endorsed recently by the World Summit on Sustainable Development (United Nations, 2002) – into practice. In pursuing this concern, the primary focus will be on how economics might help to deliver the participative and collaborative approach to environmental management envisaged by the sustainable development concept.

Part II

Theory and Method for an Economics of Collaborative Environmental Management

2

Collective Action in the Commons: The View from Mainstream Economics

> We all depend on one biosphere for sustaining our lives. Yet each community, each country, strives for survival and prosperity with little regard for its impact on others. Some consume the Earth's resources at a rate that would leave little for future generations (World Commission on Environment and Development, 1987, p27).

This excerpt from *Our Common Future* frames the challenge of environmental sustainability as a commons problem. There are many ways of thinking about environmental sustainability, but the commons framing has become widely influential. Indeed, commons problems feature in virtually all environmental problems. The far-reaching influence of 'commons thinking' on environmental policy is largely attributable to Garrett Hardin's (1968) evocative parable 'the tragedy of the commons'. Proponents of collaborative approaches to environmental management see these approaches as helping to bring about the 'mutual coercion, mutually agreed upon' in any commons setting that Hardin (ibid, p1247) prescribed as the way of averting such a tragedy (Wondolleck and Yaffee, 2000; Bryan, 2004).

The tragedy involves a resource (a pasture in Hardin's account) freely accessible to multiple human resource users (herders). The resource can be sustained if all individuals decide to limit their use (grazing). However, each individual faces a dilemma. A decision to increase use (graze more livestock on the pasture) would result in the individual obtaining all the benefits without incurring all the costs (the depletion of pasture would affect all herders). Individuals will therefore try to use up the resource before others beat them to it. Tragedy in the form of degradation of the resource thus follows inevitably, and perhaps irreversibly. Each user faces a dilemma since maximization of his or her short-term self-interest leads to a collective outcome that makes him or her worse off than could otherwise have been the case.

The mainstream economic understanding of commons problems predates Hardin's parable but is consistent with it. It seems unlikely that Hardin's simple parable would have retained such influence among non-economists had not its intellectual legitimacy been bolstered by mainstream economics. The focus in this chapter is therefore on reviewing briefly how mainstream economics understands the challenge of collective action in the commons.

The review begins in the next section by explaining how environmental and resource economists conventionally analyse commons problems, and highlighting their prediction that reliance on voluntary cooperation to solve such problems will inevitably end in the economic equivalent of Hardin's tragedy, that is, economic rent earned from the commons dissipating to zero. The subsequent section looks at how this prediction matches that made by Mancur Olson (1965) – on the basis of extending neoclassical analysis to problems of collective action more generally – for problems of collective action faced by groups with large memberships. The penultimate section discusses how Olson's neoclassical theory of collective action was reformulated in game-theoretic terms, namely as an *n*-prisoners' dilemma. The concluding section explains how the similar conclusions from environmental and resource economics, collective action theory and the *n*-prisoners' dilemma became interpreted widely as providing scientific support for Progressive assertions that social welfare in environmental commons (and other collective action) problems is best advanced by centralizing all responsibilities for providing the institutional arrangements needed to solve such problems.

Neoclassical economics of the commons

The mainstream economics of the commons, and of environmental and natural resources issues more generally, is centred on neoclassical economics. Until the 1970s, the dominant approach of neoclassical economists to policy analysis was the Pigouvian or market failure approach. This originated with Adam Smith's insight in the *Wealth of Nations*, published in 1784, that individuals maximizing their self-interest in market transactions would, under certain conditions, act as if an 'invisible hand' were guiding them to contribute to the collective good. With the publication of Arthur Pigou's *Economics of Welfare* in 1912, economists turned to specifying more rigorously these conditions. These became known as the conditions of 'perfect competition' – that is, conditions that are necessary and sufficient for market transactions to achieve Pareto efficiency. Failures to satisfy these conditions became known as 'market failures'. Identification of such failures became economists' primary method of assessing whether intervention in markets could be justified. Consistent with the Progressive vision, they presumed that the state would be responsible for undertaking any intervention judged warranted.

Environmental and natural resource economics emerged as a specialization of this Pigouvian tradition in economics. Economists in this specialization regard externalities as the main source of market failure with respect to the natural environment. Externalities arise when a market does not exist through which compensation can be exchanged for all units of goods (or bads) provided by an action. Provision of a good entails one or more of producing, restoring or maintaining it (Ostrom, 1990). Only in the case of private goods can compensation for all units provided be exchanged by way of market transactions. Private goods are characterized by complete rivalry and complete excludability. Complete rivalry exists when appropriation of units (e.g. litres) of a good (e.g. potable water) subtracts these units entirely from the stock remaining for subsequent appropriation. Complete excludability exists when the actor providing a good can prevent others from appropriating any units of the good, or can restrict appropriation to those who fully compensate the actor for the loss in benefits that the appropriation causes him or her.

All goods other than private goods are known as public goods. A pure public good is a good characterized by complete non-rivalry and complete non-excludability. A classic example is a lighthouse. Goods that are less than completely non-excludable or non-rival are known as impure public goods. Commons dilemmas are concerned with a particular class of impure public goods known as common pool resources (CPRs). These are natural resource systems (e.g. watersheds) or human-made resource systems (e.g. communal irrigation works) that produce resource units (e.g. megalitres of water) (Oakerson, 1992). Appropriation of resource units from CPRs is rival because the supply of units is replenished at a finite rate, if at all (Ostrom, 1990). Moreover, it is difficult for providers of CPRs to completely exclude others from appropriating the resource units produced as a result. This difficulty is often attributed to costliness of the existing physical or institutional means of exclusion. However, constitutional and cultural considerations can also make some exclusion options costly, at least in a political sense (e.g. privatizing a beach) (Oakerson, 1992).

It has been common for neoclassical economists, as suggested by Hardin (1968, p1244), to 'picture a pasture open to all' when modelling appropriation of CPRs. Consequently, environmental economists analysing CPRs have assumed typically that appropriation of resource units is completely non-excludable. An institutional setting of this kind is known as *res nullius*, an unowned resource system (Ciriacy-Wantrup, 1971), or 'open access'. Resource units supplied from an open access CPR are 'fugitive' in the sense that they belong to no one until they are 'captured' by any actor with the necessary means (Bromley and Cernea, 1989).

Early economic studies of open access fisheries by Gordon (1954) and Scott (1955) established the rudiments of a neoclassical economic framework for analysing simple CPRs. These rudiments can be illustrated in relation to Hardin's example of herders sharing an open access pasture. In order to simplify the exposition, it is assumed that there are only two herders (Herders A and B) in a position to place animals on the pasture, and that they each have one animal on the pasture to start with but could each increase this to two. There are direct costs of one dollar per year incurred in placing each animal on the pasture. The herders must each choose between cooperating with the other by retaining one animal on the pasture, or defecting by placing two animals on the pasture. The economic repercussions of Herder A's choice, assuming Herder B continues to cooperate, are summarized in Table 2.1.

Table 2.1 *Illustrating the neoclassical economics of an open access CPR*

	Both cooperate			Only Herder A defects			Marginal effects of Herder A defecting		
	Herder A	Herder B	Total	Herder A	Herder B	Total	Herder A	Herder B	Total
Animals placed on pasture	1	1	2	2	1	3	1	0	1
Revenue/ animal ($)	6	6		4	4		NA	NA	NA
Cost/animal ($)	1	1		1	1		NA	NA	NA
Net return/ animal ($)	5	5		3	3		NA	NA	NA
Revenue ($)	6	6	12	8	4	12	2	–2	0
Cost ($)	1	1	2	2	1	3	1	0	1
Net return ($)	5	5	10	6	3	9	1	–2	–1

If both herders cooperate, they each obtain annual revenue of $6 per animal and thus, once the direct costs are deducted, an annual net return of $5 per animal. Hence, the collective net return from the pasture is $10. Consider the incentives surrounding Herder A's choice regarding whether to defect by placing one more animal (making a total of two for her) on the pasture. If she does defect while Herder B continues to cooperate, there will then be three animals on the pasture. Pasture availability per animal falls as a result, such that the revenue from each animal declines from $6 to $4. The net return per animal declines accordingly from $5 to $3. The collective net return from the pasture (or 'economic rent') declines from $10 to $9 despite the extra animal placed on it.

Nevertheless, it is in Herder A's self-interest to defect if her private marginal revenue from placing the extra animal on the pasture exceeds her private marginal cost. Since her marginal private revenue from placing the extra animal is $2 (the difference between $8 from two animals, at $4 each, and one animal at $6) and her marginal private cost of doing so is $1, it is in Herder A's self-interest to defect. Her net private return increases by $1 despite the decline by $1 in the net collective return from the pasture. Table 2.1 reveals that the difference between Herder A's positive outcome and the negative collective outcome derives from the extra animal placed by Herder A capturing for her $2 of revenue that had gone previously to Herder B. This loss of revenue to Herder B is an indirect marginal cost brought about by Herder A's decision that Herder B, since there is open access to the pasture, is not in a position to insist on being compensated. This indirect marginal cost of Herder A's decision to defect therefore constitutes a negative externality (or 'external cost').

Herder B will, of course, not stand idly by while Herder A captures an increasing share of the finite flow of feed from the pasture, at least not if she is rationally self-interested. Indeed, given a more realistic example where more than four animals in total could be placed on the pasture, both herders would continue placing extra animals on the pasture while the marginal private revenue to each from doing so remains greater than the (assumed constant) marginal private cost. Since pasture availability per animal diminishes with more animals on the pasture, marginal private revenue will eventually, as the total number of animals keeps increasing, decline to the level of marginal private cost. At this point, the economic equivalent of Hardin's 'tragedy' – economic rent from the CPR diminishing to zero – comes to pass.

Group size and voluntary collective action

In his seminal work *The Logic of Collective Action*, Olson (1965) elaborated the conclusion from neoclassical resource economics by highlighting how the externality problem in providing CPRs and other types of 'collective goods' (goods that are incompletely excludable) becomes more difficult with increasing group size. The greater the membership of a group, he reasoned, the less will any given member share in the benefits of any contribution he or she makes to providing a collective good sought by the group (i.e. the higher will be the ratio of external benefits to private benefits). Hence, the incentive for individual members to cooperate voluntarily in providing a collective good for their group will be less the larger the group. The larger the group, therefore, the less likely is it to achieve Pareto efficient provision of the collective good, all else remaining constant.

Olson highlighted also how the chance of a group being 'privileged' – such that 'each of its members, or at least some of them, has an incentive to see that the collective good is provided, even if he has to bear the full burden of providing it himself' – would decline as group size increased (ibid, p49). The idea of groups being privileged followed from the observation that individuals with a greater interest in seeing a collective good provided typically bear 'a disproportionate share of the burden of providing the collective good' (ibid, p35). Based on this observation, the expression 'free riding' was coined to describe a situation in which group members with interest in a collective good hold back in their own provision efforts expecting that other members with a stronger interest will make up the shortfall (e.g. where one herder decides against reducing his number of animals on a shared pasture in the expectation that actions by other herders more dependent on the pasture – say, with less access to alternative income sources – will themselves reduce the collective grazing pressure sufficiently).

One further reason, concerning group organization costs (a subset of transaction costs as defined in the next chapter), was given by Olson for why we should expect an inverse relationship between group size and success in voluntary collective action. He distinguished group organization costs from the costs of providing the collective good that would remain even if the good were provided unilaterally by an individual. He observed that a group with a given number of members must have a certain minimal level of organization if it is to have any at all, and presumed that this minimal level is likely to increase with group size. The larger a group becomes, therefore, the greater the cost it faces in providing the first unit of any collective good it requires. In other words, 'the higher the hurdle that must be jumped before any of the collective good at all can be obtained' (ibid, p48).

On the basis of these arguments, Olson concluded that rational self-interested members of a large group will not contribute voluntarily to the provision of any collective good required by the group. He defined a group as large if it has sufficient members that any individual member's contribution to providing the collective good makes no discernible difference to the aggregate level of provision perceived by any other member. He asserted that no one in such a group will react positively if a member makes a contribution, or negatively if no contribution is made. Consequently, he reasoned, there is no incentive whatsoever for any single member to contribute voluntarily. This proposition became known as 'the zero contribution thesis' (Ostrom, 2000a, p137). It follows from Olson's reasoning that the conclusions of Hardin and earlier neoclassical economists in respect of CPR provision are valid only in so far as the number of CPR appropriators is large as he defined the term.

Contributions from game theory

A reformulation of Olson's neoclassical logic of collective action in game-theoretic terms offered wide scope to enrich his original insights. An early impediment to studying collective action as a game was an inability to solve for the equilibrium combination of player strategies. This impediment was overcome with discovery of the Nash equilibrium concept (Nash, 1951). A combination of various players' strategies is in Nash equilibrium if no player has an incentive to deviate from his or her strategy given that no other players deviate. There is a second solution concept for such games. A dominant strategy equilibrium exists if no one can become better off by changing strategies, regardless of the strategies chosen by other players. Such an equilibrium is always a Nash equilibrium, but the converse need not apply.

When the Nash equilibrium yields an outcome that is less than optimal for all players, the individual players are said to face a 'social dilemma' (Ostrom, 1998a). The 'prisoners' dilemma' is regarded as the canonical formulation of a social dilemma. The prisoners' dilemma is illustrated below as a two-herder commons game, following the lead of Baland and Platteau (1996, section 2.3).

The players in this version of the commons game are the same herders (Herders A and B) used earlier to illustrate the neoclassical economic approach to analysing appropriation from open access CPRs. As in that exposition: (i) the herders are each faced with a choice of how many animals to place on a given area of open access pasture; (ii) each must choose between cooperating with the other by placing one animal on the pasture or defecting by placing two animals on the pasture; and (iii) they each gain a net return of $5 if they both cooperate. Recall from the earlier exposition that the net returns to Herders A and B if the former defected while the latter cooperated were $6 and $3, respectively. This configuration of net returns applies also to this prisoners' dilemma version of the commons game. It is assumed that this configuration is reversed if Herder A cooperates while Herder B defects (so that the net returns to Herders A and

B are $3 and $6, respectively). The remaining possibility involves both herders defecting. Their net returns under this scenario are each set at $4.

This configuration of 'payoffs' (as net returns are known in game theory) is summarized in Table 2.2. The first number in each cell is the dollar payoff obtained by Herder A, and the second number is the payoff obtained by Herder B.

Table 2.2 *Payoffs for a two herder commons game as a prisoners' dilemma game*

| | | Herder B | |
		Cooperate	Defect
	Cooperate	5, 5	3, 6
Herder A			
	Defect	6, 3	4, 4

The rules of the prisoners' dilemma game require Herder A to choose either the 'cooperate' or the 'defect' row at the same time that Herder B chooses between the 'cooperate' and 'defect' columns. They are each assumed to be rationally self-interested. If Herder B cooperates, Herder A gets $5 if she also cooperates but $6 if she defects. Thus, defecting is better for Herder A in this case. If Herder B instead defects, Herder A gets $3 if she cooperates but $4 if she defects. Thus, defecting is better for the Herder A in this case as well. In fact, defecting is the best strategy regardless of the choice made by Herder B. Since the same reasoning applies to Herder B, she will also choose to defect. Individual rational self-interest thus leads to mutual defection with the herders receiving $4 each ($8 collectively). This is a dominant strategy equilibrium. However, mutual cooperation by the herders is the collectively rational (i.e. Pareto efficient) outcome, yielding $10 collectively. Individual rational self-interest thus leads to the kind of Pareto inefficient outcome that the logic of Hardin and neoclassical CPR analysts – and of Olson in respect of a large-group setting – led us to expect.

Olson's logic of large-group collective action was demonstrated to have the structure of a prisoners' dilemma game generalized from two players to n players (Hardin, 1971, 1982). With the prognosis of an n-prisoners' dilemma just as pessimistic as that for the two-person version, the diffusion of the zero contribution thesis among scholars and policy analysts gained added momentum.

The message for public consumption

Based on his neoclassical analysis of open access CPR appropriation, Gordon (1954) concluded that complete dissipation of economic rents from a CPR (equivalent in economic terms to Hardin's tragedy) could be avoided only by subjecting it to a unified directing power, either by making it the property of private individuals (referred to as 'private property') or the state. Olson (1965) concluded on the basis of his zero contribution thesis that members of a large group will cooperate to realize their collective interests only if they are induced to do so by 'selective incentives' – selective in the sense that individuals who do cooperate are treated differently from those who do not. Given that selective incentives constitute a collective good themselves, he reasoned that a large group would be unable provide this organizational capacity for itself and would therefore need to rely on some external party to provide it. Hardin's (1968, p1247) analysis of the commons dilemma led him to prescribe 'mutual coercion, mutually agreed' as the only way of aligning the interests of group members with their collective interest so that their dilemma disappears and a tragedy is averted.

Given the hold of Progressive beliefs on the bureaucratic and popular imagination, these conclusions came to be widely interpreted as adding scientific credibility to Progressive claims that the advance of human welfare is fostered most effectively by centralizing responsibilities for intervening in support of collective action. Given this bias, environmental and other commons problems came to be understood predominantly in terms of the models that had yielded these conclusions; that is, those focused on open access CPR appropriation, large-group collective action and the prisoners' dilemma.

3

Developments in Collective Action Theory for Commons Management

We saw in the previous chapter how mainstream economics concludes, in the 'zero contribution thesis', that voluntary cooperation cannot help solve problems of collective action faced by large groups in managing common pool resources. We discovered also how this conclusion was reinforced by game theoreticians modelling problems of collective action in commons management as prisoners' dilemmas, and how it became interpreted widely – given the hold of Progressive beliefs on the public imagination – as evidence that institutional solutions to commons problems can be provided only through the coercive powers of the centralized state.

The predisposition of the public imagination to arguments for centralizing responsibilities for collective action meant that a number of qualifications in these arguments were glossed over. For instance, Olson (1965) found that a large group might provide itself with collective goods through voluntary cooperation by reconfiguring itself as a federated system; that is, as a small group of small groups. For his part, Hardin (1968) made it clear that centralized coercion by the state is not a necessary part of his policy prescription for commons problems.

Meanwhile, scholars continued their attempts to understand large-group collective action in the commons. One motivation was accumulated evidence contradicting the zero provision thesis. Lichbach (1996, p6) observed, 'people vote, interest groups exist, protest organizations form, and social movements organize', and Ostrom (2000a, p138) noted extensive research demonstrating that 'individuals in all walks of life and all parts of the world voluntarily organize themselves so as to gain the benefits of trade, to provide mutual protection against risk, and to create and enforce rules that protect natural resources'.

A further motivation for continued development of collective action theory stemmed from a recognition that the Progressive position is logically incomplete. If large groups are unable to provide themselves with the institutional arrangements, or systems of selective incentives, they need to resolve their social dilemmas, how can the state – representing the largest possible group within national boundaries – provide them? To propose that the social dilemma of one large group be solved by another large group is to sweep the theoretical problem under the carpet.

In this chapter, we look at developments in theory that have contributed towards a logically complete explanation of how large-group problems of collective action are solved. We begin in the next section with the insight that problems of collective action in commons management are often modelled more appropriately as assurance problems – solvable through voluntary cooperation to the extent that group members trust one another to reciprocate their cooperation – than as prisoners' dilemmas. The following section explains how trust, itself a collective good, can come to be provided spontaneously. The penultimate section looks at the role of formal organization in bolstering the spontaneous provision of trust, and particularly at how nested systems of organization, within which state agencies comprise the higher layers, allow trust to become established across a large group. The key points of the chapter are summarized briefly in the closing section.

Commons management as an assurance problem

In seminal research grounded in game theory, Axelrod (1984) laid a way forward for understanding how large-group collective action might evolve voluntarily. He started with the canonical prisoners' dilemma game, but proposed as follows that the prisoners might escape their dilemma if the game were repeated:

> What makes it possible for cooperation to emerge is the fact that the players might meet again. This possibility means that the choice made today not only determines the outcome of this move, but can also influence the later choices of the players. The future can therefore cast a shadow back upon the present and thereby affect the current strategic situation (Axelrod, 1984, p12).

Axelrod set himself the task of discovering how cooperation might emerge among rational self-interested individuals. His method was to convene a tournament of computer-based contests in which various strategies for playing an indefinitely repeated two person prisoners' dilemma game were pitted against each other. Since indefinite repetition means that the prisoners or 'players' cannot be sure when their last interaction will occur, mutual defection is not necessarily – unlike when the number of plays is known in advance – a dominant strategy equilibrium for each play. Thus, scope remained to discover the conditions necessary for the emergence of cooperation.

By means of his tournament, Axelrod demonstrated that players following strategies of reciprocity (where cooperation continues if it is reciprocated by other players) can indeed, if the 'shadow of the future' is sufficiently strong, compete successfully with strategies of unconditional defection. According to Putnam (1993, p172), a person following a reciprocity strategy enters 'a continuing relationship of exchange that is at any time unrequited or unbalanced, but that involves mutual expectations that a benefit granted now should be repaid in the future'.

Hence, modifying the canonical single-play prisoners' dilemma game to allow indefinitely-repeated plays does allow the players to escape this dilemma. They are no longer in a situation where they must formulate their choices independently of the choices they expect each other to make. The externalities they impose on one another are now symmetric, rather than unilateral or asymmetric as they are in a prisoners' dilemma.[1] Their choices are now interdependent because the possibility of reciprocation now casts onto current choices the shadow of the future (Runge, 1981). They now face an assurance problem rather than a prisoners' dilemma. This problem arises from 'uncertainty about the expected actions of others' and is modelled appropriately as an assurance game (ibid, p604). One payoff configuration for an assurance game, illustrated in terms of the commons problem faced by the two herders featured in Tables 2.1 and 2.2, is shown in Table 3.1.

Table 3.1 *Payoffs for a two herder commons game as an assurance game*

		Herder B	
		Cooperate	Defect
Herder A	Cooperate	5, 5	3, 3.5
	Defect	3.5, 3	4, 4

Observe that each herder in this commons-game-as-an-assurance-game, in contrast to the commons-game-as-a-prisoners'-dilemma-game summarized in Table 2.2, obtains a higher payoff from cooperating (that is, placing only one animal on the shared pasture) when the other cooperates than from defecting (that is, placing two animals on the pasture) when the other cooperates. Instead of the single dominant equilibrium of mutual defection in the prisoners' dilemma version of the commons game, therefore, the assurance game version has two possible Nash equilibria – mutual cooperation or mutual defection. The one that actually results depends on whether or not the two herders are able to assure – gain trust from – one another that they will cooperate. Mutual cooperation will occur if they can, and mutual defection if they cannot.

The problem of establishing trust

The possibility of trust growing spontaneously

In the commons-game-as-an-assurance-game, tragedy in the commons is not a foregone conclusion as it is in the prisoners' dilemma version. Mutual cooperation to avert the tragedy is possible but by no means guaranteed. Realizing this possibility requires prior resolution of the problem of providing assurance or, equivalently, establishing trust. Hardin (1993, p516) character-ized the trust one person has for another as 'just the expected probability of the dependency working out well'. Trust is a key component of what has become known as 'social capital', defined by Putnam (1993, p167) as 'features of social organization, such as trust, norms, and networks, that can improve the efficiency of society by facilitating coordinated actions'.

Without trust in an assurance game, tragedy looms. As trust is a public good, its provision constitutes a second-order social dilemma. Accordingly, Chong (1991, p118) identified the risk that 'everyone will stand around waiting for others to pay the heavy start-up costs need to initiate the process [of establishing trust]'. Runge (1981) argued that it is possible for the second-order social dilemma faced by members of a group in establishing assurance, or trust, to be solved endogenously (that is, by the group itself). Prominent among endogenous solutions of this nature are strategies of reciprocity. However, as observed by Sugden (1986), players following reciprocity strategies are 'brave' since they dare to cooperate on the basis of trust that others will reciprocate. Adoption of reciprocity strategies as a solution to a group's assurance problem thus entails the third-order social dilemma of establishing enough trust to make those strategies attractive.

How then is it possible to establish enough social capital in the form of trust for reciprocity to bring about voluntary cooperation in a large-group assurance problem? In seeking to solve this puzzle, Ostrom (1998a) proposed that each individual assesses subjectively, on the basis of their reputations, the trustworthiness of those with whom they share the assurance problem. This subjective assessment is reassessed over time in the light of how others' reputations are affected by unfolding evidence of how they have practised reciprocity. Thus, trust and reciprocity mutually reinforce one another through positive feedbacks. When an individual perceives that reciprocity has increased, this strengthens her trust that others will reciprocate cooperation in the future. This strengthens the shadow of the future by raising the payoff expected from cooperating, thus augmenting her own incentive to practise reciprocity. Practising reciprocity enhances her reputation, thereby increasing others' trust in her and thus their preparedness to practise reciprocity with her. Conversely, perceptions that adoption of reciprocity has declined weaken trust that future cooperation will be reciprocated, thereby further lessening adoption. Trust, reciprocity and voluntary cooperation can thereby strengthen and fade through spontaneous social dynamics. As observed by Betts (1997, p2), 'a group can become engaged in a virtuous circle of reciprocal exchanges where trust and collaboration beget more trust and collaboration, or a vicious circle where defection and betrayal lead to more of the same'.

But how is the monitoring necessary for these positive feedbacks provided? Any increase in a group's supply of a collective good arising from the greater cooperation brought about by monitoring and its flow-on reciprocity effects is itself a collective good. Hence, providing the monitoring necessary for building trust represents a yet deeper social dilemma. It seems, therefore, that we remain stuck in a problem of infinite regress when relying on this line of rational-choice logic to explain how voluntary cooperation emerges in large groups.

Emotions and bounded rationality

Despite the failure of the foregoing logic to explain how voluntary cooperation arises in large groups, ample evidence exists that sometimes it does arise. Does this mean that voluntary cooperation in large groups arises only from irrationality among group members? No, it means that an assumption implicit in the foregoing logic about human rationality in large-group social dilemmas is inappropriate. The implicit assumption is that an individual's choice is rational if it maximizes his or her self-interest. According to E. O. Wilson (1999, p203), this assumption is a product of 'folk psychology... shot through with misconceptions'. A more realistic conception of human rationality, he argued, would recognize that the human brain is almost universally regarded by biologists to have evolved through natural selection. From this standpoint:

> The human brain bears the stamp of 400 million years of trial and error... In the final step the brain was catapulted to a radically new level, equipped for language and culture. Because of its ancient pedigree, however, it could not be planted like a new computer into an empty cranial space... The new brain had to be jury-rigged in steps within and around the old brain... The result was human nature animated with animal craftiness and emotion, combining the passion of politics and art with rationality, to create a new instrument of survival (Wilson, 1999, p116).

According to Wilson and others contributing to the disciplines of human sociobiology and evolutionary psychology, biological evolution has left animals and humans innately prepared to learn certain behaviours, and innately predisposed against learning other behaviours. Given the evolutionary history of humanity, they reason, it is reasonable to suppose that innate predispositions to learn cooperative behaviours remain an important ingredient of human nature. Human evolution occurred mostly during the three-million-year long Pleistocene era that ended about 10,000 years ago, a period during which humans lived in groups of hunter-gatherers. Group members depended on each other for solving many everyday problems of collective action like mutual protection (Barkow et al, 1992). Ostrom (2000a, p143) proposed accordingly that '[t]hose of our ancestors who solved these problems most effectively, and learned how to recognize who was deceitful and who was a trustworthy reciprocator, had a selective advantage over those who did not'. It is plausible then to suppose that humans today are biologically predisposed to learn and apply reciprocity and other strategies that help them to cope with collective action problems. Indeed, considerable evidence has been accumulated in support of this proposition (Cosmides and Tooby, 1992).

Consistent with this view, Frank (1990) argued that emotions evolved biologically as a means for humans to escape the problem of infinite regress confronting them in assurance problems if their rationality restricts them always to maximizing self-interest. According to Elster (1998), emotions are triggered by beliefs. The stronger the belief, therefore, the more emotionally will it be expressed or followed. In Frank's account, emotions have arisen because commitments (e.g. promises or threats) that would not be trusted if made by a self-interest maximizer *can* become trusted if made by an individual who demonstrates emotionally that she is prepared to place such commitments above maximizing her self-interest.

These ideas complement an older literature arguing that human rationality is bounded by cognitive constraints (Hayek, 1945; Simon, 1955). In this view, people are incapable of calculating optimal solutions to complex problems, even with complete information. Rather, they choose at some level to 'satisfice' by setting an arbitrary limit on the range of possibilities explored and then making a choice from this subset. Elster (1998) argued, referring to the passage below, that people make these choices by drawing on their emotions:

> [The] role of emotion is to supply the insufficiency of reason... For a variable but always limited time, an emotion limits the range of information that an organism will take into account, the inferences actually drawn from a potential infinity, and the set of live options from which it will choose (de Sousa, 1987, p195).

Viewing rationality as bounded in this way highlights the importance of distinguishing between the world as it 'really' is and how people interpret it subjectively. North (1990, p23) emphasized accordingly the important role that ideology and mental models play in institutiorn al choices. Denzau and North (1994, p4) defined ideology as 'the shared framework of mental models that groups of individuals possess' and mental models as 'the internal representations that individual cognitive systems create to interpret the environment'. Mental models are synonymous with belief systems. Those mental models giving people good outcomes in particular kinds of day-to-day decision problems are known as heuristics.

Ostrom, Gardner and Walker (1994a) proposed that individuals faced with large-group problems of collective action use heuristics to learn about their complex decision situation. They argued that individuals, lacking both the information and cognitive capacity to calculate all future contingencies and decide once and for all on a single strategy, adapt their heuristics sequentially as they learn about their decision situation including about the other people sharing the problem. Indeed, accumulated evidence from 'laboratory experiments', designed to study how humans faced with collective action problems actually behave, indicates that a substantial proportion of the population drawn upon in these experiments use a heuristic of reciprocity when facing such problems – even when these experiments are in the form of single-play games with isolated anonymous players (ibid).

Social norms often 'result from (and crystallize) the gradual emergence of a consensus' (Posner and Rasmussen, 1999, p370). If conditions are conducive to adoption of reciprocity heuristics escalating by means of a mutually reinforcing relationship with trust formation, then reciprocity may become common enough to acquire the status of a social norm. A social norm is 'a rule that is neither promulgated by an official source, such as a court or legislature, nor enforced by the threat of legal sanctions, yet is regularly complied with' (Posner, 1997, p365). Social norms are also known as informal institutions. Institutions are 'generally agreed-upon and enforced prescriptions that require, forbid, or permit specific actions for more than a single individual'

(Schlager and Ostrom, 1992, p250). They are equivalent to what Olson (1965) called systems of selective incentives.

The social norms learned by individuals depend on their cultural milieu. This explains why reliance on particular types of norms, including reciprocity norms, varies considerably across cultures, across individuals and families within a culture, within individuals across different types of situations, and across time within any particular situation (Ostrom, 1998a).

Establishing trust through verbal and face-to-face communication

The discussion until now has proceeded on the assumption – introduced first when discussing the prisoners' dilemma game – that individuals sharing an assurance problem are unable to communicate verbally prior to making their choices. This assumption is clearly unrealistic for many assurance problems where there is scope for each player to communicate verbally with at least some other players.

This scope can allow a group facing a collective action problem to reduce its costs of organizing considerably, including in reaching a shared understanding of the problem and agreeing to a solution that clarifies the particular kind of cooperation expected from each group member. It may not be immediately apparent to all individuals that they are caught in a collective action problem, and consequently that they could do better for themselves by cooperating than by acting independently. In so far as individuals have internalized a norm for promise-keeping, promises to cooperate that individuals make in the process of agreeing to a solution to their shared problem can add significantly to their likelihood of actually cooperating. When there are repeated opportunities for communication, moreover, group members are able to revise their original agreement if it proves to be unworkable or ineffective in its existing form (Ostrom, 1998a).

Consistently in collective-action laboratory experiments, cooperation levels have been considerably higher when communication occurs face-to-face compared with other media (Ostrom et al, 1994a; Sally, 1995). On the basis of observed behaviour in such experiments, Ostrom (1998a) offered two explanations for why cooperation levels are higher when communication occurs face-to-face. The first was that face-to-face communication enhances individuals' ability to assess others' reputations for trustworthiness as well as establish their own reputations. This accords with Wilson's (1999, p174) observation that:

> If all verbal communication were stripped away, we would still be left with a rich paralanguage that communicates most of our basic needs: body odors, blushing and other telltale reflexes, facial expressions, postures, gesticulations, and nonverbal vocalizations, all of which, in various combinations and often without conscious intent, compose a veritable dictionary of mood and intention.

The second explanation was that chastising defectors and praising cooperators, which becomes possible in repeated-play experiments with communication allowed after each round, has added emotional force when exercised face-to-face. The efficacy of applying selective incentives through social approval and disapproval thereby is increased – even when compliance with an agreement can be monitored only for the group in aggregate rather than individually for each of its members. A further explanation, based again on behaviour observed repeatedly in laboratory experiments, is that face-to-face communication can promote 'group identity' and thereby make group members sufficiently more regarding of each other's welfare that they become more likely to cooperate with each other (Dawes et al, 1990; Gächter and Fehr, 1999).

Multiplex relationships

In reality, each person faces a steady succession of assurance problems. At least in smaller communities, therefore, it is likely that any given individual will share a variety of such problems with a common group of others. In his study of the governance of cattle trespass problems in a county of California, for instance, Ellickson (1991) noted that farmers typically deal with one another on a variety of fronts, including water supply, controlled burns, fence repairs, social events and staffing the volunteer fire brigade. He referred to such overlapping relationships as 'multiplex', in contrast to 'simplex' relationships between people who interact on a single front only.

An advantage of groups characterized by multiplex relationships, or 'dense social networks', is that individuals are likely to have more 'repeat plays of assurance games' with one another than would be the case if most relationships were simplex. This advantage has a number of aspects. First, the greater interconnectedness of 'games' strengthens the shadow of the future for individuals. This is because defection in any single play of one game puts at risk benefits not only from others cooperating with them in future plays of that particular game but in other games as well. Second, the greater frequency of repeat plays increases opportunities for the feedback that individuals require to establish and maintain their own reputations and assess the trustworthiness of others. Third, since trust is strengthened the more it is used, the greater number of reinforcing encounters in dense networks tends to make norms of reciprocity more robust. Finally, denser networks allow greater flexibility in practising reciprocity – people can more easily reciprocate cooperation in accordance with their own endowments and preferences rather than on a strict 'like for like' basis.

Leadership

Opportunities for communication can strengthen the contribution that leadership can play in facilitating the feedback within large groups necessary for building trust. Leadership is distinct from authority since following a leader is a voluntary, rather than a coerced, activity of the followers (Hermalin, 1998).

Wallis and Dollery (1995, p41) proposed that the essential function of leaders is to facilitate 'the convergence of the hopes of their followers into a "vision" which they can share in common'. Hope is an emotion, and is therefore triggered by belief. In this case, the belief relates to a 'person's image of what his or her own life, and the community in which this life is situated, could become' through participating in a collective quest (ibid, p39). This belief, and the emotions it evokes, allows individuals to savour in advance the realization of a shared vision.

To the extent that the leader of a group can articulate a vision that is consonant with its members' hopes, leaders can simplify greatly the feedback between members necessary to achieve agreement that there is a need to cooperate and that cooperation should take a certain form. The lower then will be the hurdle of organizational costs faced by large groups seeking to undertake collective action.

Feedback as a by-product of everyday social interaction

The activity of providing feedback within a group does not only involve costs, as the foregoing discussion might be taken to suggest. Humans are social creatures and often gain considerable satisfaction from the feedback processes of monitoring one another, sharing what they have seen and heard, and providing social rewards and punishments. The greater this satisfaction, the lower the net cost to individuals of partaking in such processes. Jacobs (1992, p56) captured this phenomenon vividly in the context of US inner city neighbourhoods:

> The trust of a city street is formed over time from many, many little sidewalk contacts. It grows out of people stopping by at the bar for a beer, getting advice from the grocer and giving advice to the newsstand man, comparing opinions with other customers at the bakery and nodding hello to the two boys drinking pop on the stoop, eyeing the girls while being called for dinner, admonishing the children... The sum of such casual, public contact at a local level... is a feeling for the public identity of people, a web of public respect and trust.

Jacobs' observations of urban street life highlight an insight now usually attributed to Granovetter (1973). He observed that 'strong' interpersonal ties tend to be less important than 'weak' ties in sustaining community cohesion and collective action. Strong ties generally occur among people who share common bonds. Weak ties tend to be more instrumental, and enable the building of 'social bridges' between groups that less obviously share common bonds. Hence, weak ties are indispensable for integrating individuals within large groups.

After illustrating how weak ties can generate trust sufficient for a neighbourhood of strangers to function effectively as a community, Jacobs proceeded to describe how such ties can also enable collective action to emerge spontaneously at the higher level of districts. For this to occur requires a particular type of weak ties, namely:

working relationships among people, usually leaders, who enlarge their local public life beyond the neighborhoods of streets and specific organizations or institutions and form relationships with people whose roots and backgrounds are in entirely different constituencies, so to speak… It takes surprisingly few [of these] hop-skip people, relative to a whole population, to weld a district into a real Thing (Jacobs, 1992, p134).

The role of formal organization

The foregoing explains how voluntary cooperation in solving large-group problems of collective action, such as those often faced by CPR appropriators, sometimes emerges and grows spontaneously. By no means does this deny an important role for formal organization. In this section we explore how formal organization can help CPR appropriators solve the large-group problems of collective action they share.

Endogenous formal organization

Institutional arrangements provided formally by formally established organizations are typically needed in large-group situations to bolster the shadow of the future – by increasing the likelihood of defections being identified and punished – sufficiently so that the defection rate does not exceed a threshold over which trust and cooperation begin to unravel in a vicious circle. In the case of large groups, therefore, formal organizational (or 'vertical') sources of trust are often important in complementing spontaneous (or 'horizontal') sources.

This does not mean that large groups need to depend entirely on external organizations to provide them with formal institutional arrangements. Indeed, there is now considerable empirical evidence that large groups can sometimes, with little or no external intervention, provide themselves with formal organizational systems capable of designing, implementing, monitoring and enforcing such institutions. Impressive evidence of such 'endogenous' provision of organizational capacity has come from field research of cases where CPR appropriators have developed and maintained formal organizations to resolve their social dilemmas. In *Governing the Commons*, for instance, Elinor Ostrom (1990) studied a range of cases involving small-scale CPRs (e.g. forests, irrigation systems and inshore fisheries) where groups of up to 15,000 persons – that Olson would have considered to be large and thus incapable of successfully providing themselves with formal organizational arrangements – had been organizing themselves formally across multiple generations.

A centrepiece of Ostrom's work has been the identification of 'design principles' for enduring, self-governing CPR organizations – seven that apply to all such organizations, plus an eighth principle that applies to larger, more complex cases. A design principle means here an essential element or condition that helps to account for the success of these organizations in sustaining the

CPRs and gaining long-term compliance of appropriators to the institutions in place. These design principles can be viewed as necessary, although usually not sufficient, conditions to be met for the costs of CPR appropriators organizing themselves formally to be low enough that the assurance problem in covering these costs is not insurmountable.

Ostrom's (ibid, p90) eighth design principle reads: 'Appropriation, provision, monitoring, enforcement, conflict resolution, and governance activities [of long-enduring CPR organizations] are organized in multiple layers of nested enterprises'. This design principle has attracted considerable interest, especially from scholars and policy analysts concerned with promoting self-organization of large groups in complex societies. It recognizes that complex CPR problems, for which formal organization in a single step typically involves prohibitive organizational costs, are often decomposable into sequences of smaller problems – and that the costs of formal organizational solutions to some of these smaller problems may not present intractable assurance problems.

Once a formal organizational base is established for smaller problems, the opportunity to 'piggy-back' on it to address an assurance problem that is incrementally more challenging may allow this problem to be resolved endogenously when otherwise the hurdle of the costs of organizing would be prohibitive. This way organizational capacity can accumulate endogenously through 'the incremental self-transformations that frequently are involved in the process of supplying institutions' (Ostrom, 1990, p190).

Thus, an elaborate multi-layered system of nested enterprises can be the eventual result of larger, more inclusive organizational units emerging from, and then 'nesting' – in the sense of complementing rather than absorbing or sidelining – smaller, more exclusive units that manage to self-organize sooner. Smaller organizations thus become a part of a more inclusive system without giving up their essential autonomy. This proposition is consistent with Olson's (1965) suggestion that a large group's inability to provide itself with a public good might be overcome by restructuring the group as a federation of smaller groups. Unlike Ostrom, however, he did not explain how such a federation could emerge given the large-group problem of collective action this would entail.

This explanation of large-group organization portrays the various levels of government as the higher layers of a nested polycentric system. In the case of the Spanish *huertas*, for instance, 'irrigators are organized on the basis of three or four nested levels, all of which are then also nested in local, regional, and national governmental jurisdictions' (Ostrom, 1990, p102). Such a system has been characterized in more abstract terms as one in which:

> Each unit may exercise considerable independence to make and enforce rules within a circumscribed scope of authority for a specified geographical area. In a polycentric system, some units are general-purpose governments, whereas others may be highly specialized... Self-organized resource governance systems, in such a system, may be special districts, private associations, or

parts of local government. These are nested in several levels of general-purpose governments that also provide civil equity as well as criminal courts (Ostrom, 1999, p528).

Moreover, this explanation of large-group collective action offers a coherent alternative to the logically incomplete prescription by Progressives that the state – a large-group public good – should intervene to redress the supposed inability of large groups of citizens to provide themselves with collective goods. This coherent alternative entails the state ceasing to view itself as a Leviathan and re-inventing itself such that it complements, rather than displaces or absorbs, self-organizing capacities at smaller scales of social interaction. In other words, it involves the state contributing towards large-group collective action *in partnership with*, not just on behalf of, these lower-level units of formal organization.

In no way does this explanation of success in large-group collective action deny a vital role for the state in facilitating the provision of large-group public goods. As North (1990, p58) has argued:

> Quite complex exchange can be realized by creating third-party enforcement via voluntary institutions that lower transaction costs about the other party; ultimately, however, viable impersonal exchange that would realize the gains from trade inherent in the technologies of modern interdependent economies requires institutions that can enforce agreements by the threat of coercion. The transaction costs of a purely voluntary system of third-party enforcement in such an environment would be prohibitive. In contrast there are immense scale economies in policing and enforcing agreements by a polity that acts as a third party and uses coercion to enforce agreements.

For Wells and Lynch (2000, p133), the concept of large-group collective action in environmental management as a system of nested enterprises gives much-needed contemporary substance to the notion of civil society that is central to John Locke's notion of a social contract, and helps also to clarify the role of the state as the protector of this realm. From this standpoint, they argued:

> The state is simply the most inclusive social commons regime around. It has no special, and no unique powers. Sovereignty is often pointed to here as the mark of such uniqueness and interpreted in authoritarian terms, but in the Lockean framework... [s]overeignty means rather, first, that the state should function as a 'final court of appeal', and second, that it defends and furthers the formation of those social commons regimes necessary to deal with our emerging environmental problems.

Establishing and maintaining vertical trust

Endogenous organizational solutions to problems of collective action involve creating a specific position responsible for supplementing the spontaneous emergence of trust among group members. Such a position may be filled by one or more group members (e.g. as a committee or in rotation) or by an external party. In any event, the occupant of such a position is regarded as a 'third party' in the sense that the occupant is supposed to treat all group members impartially while providing formalized monitoring, sanctioning and enforcement services.

By introducing a third party to help solve an existing assurance problem, however, a group creates for itself a new assurance problem. Its 'horizontal' assurance problem – between group members – may be solved more success-fully, but not without introducing 'vertical' assurance problems between group members and the third party. As Putnam (1993, p165) remarked: 'For third-party enforcement to work, the third party must itself be trustworthy'. Only with trust in the third party will group members regard his or her decisions as legitimate and feel responsibility to abide by them.

Defection by the state in a vertical assurance problem, intentionally or not, is called 'government failure' by economists. Even if those who rule at the highest level are determined that the state not defect, the difficulty remains of ensuring that others within state agencies cooperate with them. As Arrow (1974, p72) observed: 'The control mechanisms are themselves organizations, composed of people. Their use to enforce authority is itself an exercise of authority'. This kind of challenge represents a type of 'agency problem', characterized by Wallis and Dollery (1999, p69) as follows:

> A principal–agent relationship comes into being whenever a principal delegates authority to an agent whose behaviour has an impact on the principal's welfare... By delegating authority to an agent, the principal economises on scarce resources by adopting an informed and able agent, but simultaneously takes on the risk that, since the interests of the principal and agent will never be identical, the agent may fail to maximise the wealth of the principal.

A social contract may be understood accordingly as entailing citizens, as principals, engaging the state as their common agent to help solve their problems of collective action. They delegate to the state various powers on the condition that the powers are used for this purpose only. However, this inevitably provides considerable scope for these powers to be used for other purposes. Hence, the problems of collective action faced by citizens are lessened by entering a social contract with the state only to the extent that they trust the state not to fail them. The more that this trust is lacking, the less will citizens judge it in their individual self-interest to cooperate with interventions the state claims are designed to help them, and the greater consequently will be the need for state coercion to help citizens attain a given level of cooperation with one another. Lichbach (1996, pp216–217) encapsulated the implications of this as follows: 'Force is therefore never sufficient to maintain social order because if enough people disobey orders, the orders become too costly to enforce'.

Declining citizen trust in the state was identified in Chapter 1 as one important reason for the emergence of the collaborative vision for environmental management. On the basis of data from *World Value* surveys carried out in 1981–1983, 1990–1993 and 1995–1997, Norris (1999b) found indeed that public confidence in the core institutions of representative government – including parties, parliaments and governments – had fallen in most established and newer democracies. The economic repercussions of these trends are highlighted by the further finding that trust in government is positively associated with willingness to obey the law voluntarily (Norris, 1999a).

Berger and Neuhaus (1977, p3) proposed that the problem of diminishing citizen trust in the state – or at least that part of it due to growing cultural distance between public and private life – might be mitigated by policy makers recognizing the vital contribution of the 'mediating structures' of civil society to making individuals 'more "at home" in society, and the political order ... more "meaningful"'. This would follow from these organizations, including neighbourhood groups and voluntary associations, having both a private face and a public face. In terms of Ostrom's (1990) suggestion that we organize large-group collective action for managing natural resources in multiple layers of nested enterprises, the enterprises at each level can usefully be thought of as mediating structures – making it more possible to grow vertical trust in the part of the organizational system where the enterprises are situated by breaking into more achievable steps what otherwise may be an alienating cultural distance for citizens.

Organizational nesting of this kind provides increased scope for making formal institutional interventions consonant with the informal institutions, including social norms, already at work in particular settings such that 'informal processes of social control largely subsume the cost of monitoring and enforcement' (Nee, 1998, p88). Without such consonance, the prevailing norms can be expected to survive as 'opposition norms' that increase the costs of monitoring and enforcing the formal institutions considerably (ibid). Thus 'revolutionary change is never as revolutionary as its supporters desire' (North, 1994, p366).

This is not to presume that it is easy to know which way the grain of informal culture runs in particular local settings. Without such knowledge, 'it is easy, almost inadvertently, to destroy social arrangements which represent substantial past investments with enormous potential' (Day, 1998, p103). Clearly, the best source of knowledge about the aspirations and informal institutions of a group is its members. The likelihood of formal interventions helping rather than hindering collective action by a large group will be enhanced consequently by enabling group members to participate inclusively in planning the interventions and implementing them. Organizational nesting can facilitate this inclusive participation by enabling opportunities for participation at any level to be designed and managed by those most familiar with the cultural and other factors affecting incentives to participate.

The challenge of collaboration

As reviewed in Chapter 2, the logic of mainstream economics indicates that large-group collective action in solving commons problems can succeed only when responsibilities for providing institutional solutions to these problems are assigned to a monocentric organizational system driven by the coercive powers of the state. It follows from this logic that collaborative approaches to solving commons problems, wherein responsibilities for providing institutional solutions are shared across a polycentric organizational system, and where coordination across the system relies substantially on voluntary cooperation, are doomed to failure.

In this chapter we saw that this logic is incomplete since it cannot explain how the state, a large-group collective good, was and continues to be provided. An alternative logic was presented, one consistent with the evidence that voluntary cooperation often contributes significantly towards success in large-group collective action. This alternative logic recognizes that there are limits to coercing cooperation due to the costs involved, and that a state's capacity to solve all the large-group commons problems faced by its citizens depends, therefore, on its capacity to develop and implement solutions in collaboration with civil society – that is, in ways that 'nest' within polycentric organizational systems the voluntary problem-solving efforts of citizens that are made possible by trust and reciprocity.

Collaboration between the state and civil society may well be essential if we are to manage our burgeoning environmental problems within our means, but we know already that it is far from simple. The next chapter offers an economic perspective on the complexity of the institutional choices involved in organizing environmental management collaboratively, and presents an economic framework suitable for analysing institutional choices of such complexity.

An Economics for Collaborative Environmental Management

[T]o properly consider and evaluate collaboration we must...
ask the question, 'As compared to what?' So the question is not
'Can this be accomplished without flaw?' but rather 'Is this better
than our alternatives, and can we make it better?' (Bryan, 2004,
pp893–894).

An economic framework capable of addressing this question, in order to engage
reasonably with the complexity of institutional choices entailed by the
collaborative vision for environmental management, is developed in this
chapter. We begin by revisiting the comparative institutions approach to
economic analysis that arose from the Coasean challenge to the market-failure
tradition in neoclassical welfare economics. The economic framework
presented here constitutes a more realistic application of this approach than
developed previously. In the following section, we look at the limitations of the
deductive method of comparative statics for analysing complex institutional
choices; that is, choices with outcomes determined significantly by increasing
returns (positive feedbacks). We then turn to considering the path dependency
implications of complex institutional choices, and the suggestion from
complexity economists that an inductive method be applied to account for these
implications. Also explored here are the parallels between this suggestion and
the growing societal consensus that complex environmental problems are best
solved through adaptive management. In the subsequent section, the value of
the 'adaptive efficiency' concept advanced by the economic historian Douglass
North (1990) is considered in respect of providing economists with a platform
from which they might contribute towards cross-disciplinary efforts to apply the
concept of adaptive management. In the penultimate section, a conceptual
framework for applying the comparative institutions approach to support
pursuit of the collaborative vision through adaptive management is developed.
The chapter ends with some comments on the challenges that lie ahead in
getting economists to adopt this framework.

The comparative institutions approach to economic analysis

As discussed in Chapter 2, the market-failure or Pigouvian approach to policy
analysis was dominant among mainstream neoclassical economists until the

1970s or so. This dominance began to wane when Ronald Coase (1960), a neoclassical economist, highlighted an internal inconsistency in the Pigouvian logic of equating market failure with Pareto inefficiency. He observed that the ideal of perfect competition against which Pigouvians diagnose market failures assumes zero 'transaction costs' – the costs of negotiating, exchanging and enforcing property rights and of establishing, changing and enforcing the institutions underpinning property rights. Property rights confer an ability to exercise choices over a good (Allen, 1991).

Coase demonstrated that externalities will be eliminated spontaneously in a neoclassical world of zero transaction costs with all economic agents maximizing their self interest. The economic rent that would be dissipated due to the externalities would immediately be captured by agents able costlessly to negotiate a new property rights configuration that solves the excludability problems responsible for the externalities (i.e. 'internalizes the externalities'). The same Pareto efficient assignment of property rights would result regardless of how property rights are assigned originally. Given perfect competition and self-interest-maximizing agents, therefore, the Pigouvian rationale for government intervention is redundant. In the real world of positive transaction costs, moreover, Coase demonstrated that spontaneous property right negotiations will still ensure that all Pareto relevant externalities are internalized. Any existing configuration of property rights is therefore Pareto efficient. In this case, too, no market failure case for government intervention can be justified.

With the logic of the market failure approach discredited, Demsetz (1969, p1) proposed that government intervention be assessed according to a 'comparative institutions approach' that would 'attempt to assess which alternative real institutional arrangement seems best able to cope with the economic problem'. With this approach, evidence of market failure is not sufficient to justify intervention. It is necessary in addition to specify the institutional arrangements proposed to replace the status quo and to *realistically* assess the likelihood of the proposed arrangements delivering a better solution to the economic problem.

This call for economists to engage more realistically with the complexity of institutional choices by comparing 'actual with actual' was muted considerably, however, by the ongoing priority within mainstream economics of maintaining the predictive precision needed to fulfil Progressive expectations of a scientific discipline. As a result, the comparative institutions approach was simplified by environmental and resource economists to the extent that government intervention was considered justified when existing property rights depart from an ideal of 'non-attenuation'. One attribute of a non-attenuated system of property rights is that exclusive rights to all property are assigned to *individuals*. Proponents of non-attenuated property rights as an ideal held that its full realization would yield a socially preferable outcome through ensuring Pareto efficiency (Randall, 1981) when in fact, as explained above, any existing configuration of property rights must already be Pareto efficient if economic agents are all assumed to maximize self interest. Nevertheless, commitment to this ideal boosted the Progressive scientific credentials of mainstream economics since, as explained in Chapter 1, economic theory justifies precise predictions of aggregate economic behaviour only where this behaviour arises from individuals acting in accordance with independently formed preferences. Admitting the possibility that social welfare might sometimes be greater with property rights assigned to groups rather than individuals would have exposed economists to analysing institutional options, the consequences of which they could not precisely predict.

Despite the Coasean critique of Pigouvian logic, therefore, mainstream economics continued to view public policy as limited effectively to a choice between the 'visible hand' of the state (seen now as having a crucial role in transforming existing attenuated systems of property rights into non-attenuated systems) and the 'invisible hand' of the market. This choice is equivalent in property rights terminology to a choice between systems of government property and individual property. A system of government property prevails when enforceable property rights are held by government, whereas a system of individual property exists when exclusive property rights are held by individuals (Ostrom et al, 1999a).

Aside from the reason that the aggregate outcomes of institutional options involving common (or group) property systems – where property rights are shared by a finite number of group members who are able to exclude non-members (ibid.) – cannot be precisely predicted, mainstream economics also dismissed common property as a feasible institutional option on the basis that the zero provision thesis predicts (we now know incorrectly) that a group of any significant size will invariably be unable to solve the problems of collective action involved in establishing and enforcing the institutions needed for members to fulfil their common interests in the property.

Perhaps the strongest argument for neoclassical economists emphasizing individual property at the expense of common property originated in another tradition of economic thought. In advancing his evolutionary theory of economics, Alchian (1950) acknowledged that economic agents ordinarily make choices subject to limited information and bounded rationality. Rather than surveying all feasible alternatives and then calculating the choice which maximizes satisfaction of an objective, he argued that each agent typically satisfices with a limited search. The more complex and thus uncertain the decision environment, accordingly, the more likely it is that the efficient choice will be located by a group whose members conduct their own independent searches than by a group that conducts a single search for all its members.

Based on this reasoning, leading economists like Milton Friedman (1953) concluded that efficiency in a complex dynamic world is tracked most success-fully by decentralizing property systems as far as possible; namely to the level of individual property at which markets operate. The number of agents searching for the efficient option is thereby maximized. Markets also maximize competition between the agents performing the searches – ensuring that inefficient options are 'weeded out' in a process of competitive selection so that supposedly only the most efficient ones survive. This reasoning became influential among environmental and resource economists, especially due to the efforts of 'free-market environmentalists' (Anderson and Leal, 1991). As explained below, however, this reasoning is often misguided when applied to institutional choices.

For these various reasons, much of the promise of the comparative institutions approach to increase the sophistication with which economists analyse complex institutional choices remains to be fulfilled. As Challen (2000) has observed, it is common in environmental policy settings to find government and individual systems of property co-existing with each other as well as with common property systems and elements of open access (i.e. a lack of any kind of enforced property system). He illustrated such a nested system of property rights with an account of how surface water use by irrigators in Australia's Murray Darling Basin is regulated. To be sure, all water for irrigation in this setting is appropriated within systems of individual property. Nevertheless, the term 'individual property' fails to do justice to the complexity of property arrangements affecting this use. Only a subset of all the rights ultimately affecting irrigators' use of water are included in the property rights held by individuals, and these rights are subordinate to common property rights shared by irrigators, to government property rights held by the relevant governments within the Australian federal system, and to rights assigned to the system of inter-governmental common property established subject to the Murray Darling Basin Agreement of 1992. Given the interdependence of these different systems of property rights, analysis in such a complex setting only of how government and individual property systems affect surface water use would clearly run a significant risk of reaching inaccurate conclusions.

Indeed, the preoccupation in institutional analysis with government and individual property systems means that existing common property systems, even highly successful ones, can become effectively invisible to analysts. Ostrom (1999, p520) mentioned a case in the Chitwan valley in Nepal, for instance, where:

> an Asian Development Bank team of irrigation engineers recommended a large loan to build a dam across the Rapti River to enable the farmers there to irrigate their crops. What the engineering design team did not see were the 85 farmer-managed irrigation systems that already existed in the valley and had achieved relatively high performance.

The political economy as a mechanistic system

The failure in mainstream economics to follow through with the comparative institutions approach, at least beyond considering market-based institutional interventions (involving individual property systems) as the only viable alternative to state interventions (involving government property systems), derives ultimately from its reluctance to relinquish the predictive precision, and hence Progressive scientific credibility, it obtains from analysing the political economy as if it were a machine – that is, as a system characterized by constant relationships between constant parts. It is this commitment to mechanistic

collaborative governance is always being made and re-made

analysis that explains the aversion in mainstream economics to considering institutional options involving the allocation of property rights to groups, both because: (a) constant preference rankings for groups cannot be derived from the preference rankings of their members, at least without retreating from classical liberalism's commitment to protecting individuals' rights of privacy; and (b) mechanistic analysis, as exemplified by the neoclassical economics of collective goods provision (see Chapter 2), cannot explain how members of groups of any significant size would organize themselves to utilize effectively any property rights allocated to them in common.

The method of mechanistic analysis used in mainstream economics is known now as 'comparative statics', abbreviated from 'comparative static equilibrium analysis'. It was introduced by Alfred Marshall (1920, p304, original emphasis), one of the founders of neoclassical economics, who proposed that complex economic dynamics in the real world be simplified for analytical purposes as follows:

> The element of time... makes it necessary for man with his limited powers to go step by step; breaking up a complex question, studying one bit at a time, and at last combining his partial solutions to a more or less complete solution of the whole riddle. In breaking it up, he segregates those disturbing causes, whose wanderings happen to be inconvenient, for the time in a pound called *Caeteris Paribus*. The study of some group of tendencies is isolated by the assumption *other things being equal*: the existence of other tendencies is not denied, but their disturbing effect is neglected for a time.

As Marshall recognized, the possibility of each set of economic circumstances having a unique equilibrium follows from the law of diminishing returns. According to this law, as the quantities of a variable factor (e.g. labour) applied to given quantities of a fixed factor (e.g. land) continues to increase, the benefit from the marginal unit of variable factor applied will eventually decrease. If one producer is advantaged more than others by a disturbance to an existing equilibrium (e.g. a change in the weather lifts the demand for her product more than for others' products), for instance, the operation of this law means the returns from exploiting the advantage by employing additional units of variable factors will eventually disappear. The behaviour of producers thus settles into a new equilibrium. Diminishing returns therefore act as a self-dampening, or negative-feedback, mechanism.

When the method of comparative statics is applied, therefore, a single constant relationship exists between cause (e.g. a particular institutional intervention) and effect (e.g. provision level for a particular collective good). This makes precise prediction (at least with a known probability distribution) a credible aspiration, especially when the knowledge requirements for such prediction are reduced to a manageable level by exploiting the 'other things being equal' strategy to confine the analysis to a limited portion of the whole relevant system.

Despite the analytical precision of comparative statics, Marshall was emphatic that this method be used only temporarily until economic dynamics could be analysed more realistically. He reasoned as follows, that the errors resulting from this method would be especially serious in respect of long-term problems (of which pursuit of the collaborative vision for environmental management would certainly be one):

> [V]iolence is required for keeping broad forces in the pound of *Caeteris Paribus* during, say, a whole generation, on the ground that they have only an indirect bearing on the question at hand. For even indirect influences may produce great effects in the course of a generation, if they happen to act cumulatively; and it is not safe to ignore them even provisionally in a practical problem without special study (Marshall, 1920, p315).

Marshall referred to the dynamic process of effects acting cumulatively as one of 'increasing returns'. Economists now also refer to this kind of process as 'cumulative causation', which 'describes a relationship between an initial change in an independent variable and the dependent variable, whereby the dependent variable in turn causes a change in the formerly independent variable in the same direction as the initial movement' (Schmid, 2004, p112). We can see, therefore, that the positive feedbacks identified in the previous chapter linking trust, reciprocity and cooperation are synonymous with increasing returns.

When the dynamics of a problem feature increasing returns, Marshall warned, the risks of comparative statics providing inaccurate answers are greatest. One of his reasons for concern regarding the application of comparative statics to long-term problems subject to increasing returns is that this method predicts a single equilibrium outcome when in fact there may be multiple possible equilibria 'any one of which is equally consistent with the general circumstances of the market, and any one of which if once reached would be stable, until some great disturbance occurred' (Marshall, 1920, p665). We can now see how the failure of comparative statics to account for the increasing return dynamics linking trust, reciprocity and cooperation – and also for the kinds of random events, like emergence of leadership, that determine which of multiple possible equilibria prevails – renders it incapable of explaining how large groups sometimes contribute endogenously towards the provision of collective goods (e.g. common property systems).

The political economy as a complex adaptive system

Despite Marshall's warning, comparative statics became entrenched as the core method of mainstream economics. This state of affairs remained largely unquestioned until 'complexity economists' like David (1985) and W. Brian Arthur (1988, 1989) came to formalize Marshall's concerns in what became known as the 'path dependency' literature. Indeed, the following character-ization by Altman, 2000 (pp128–129) of the fundamental argument in this literature echoes Marshall's argument closely:

> [T]he free market typically generates suboptimal long run equilibrium solutions to a variety of economic problems and the probability of suboptimal equilibrium outcomes increases where increasing returns (positive feedbacks) prevail... This argument is couched in a discussion of there being possible multiple equilibrium solutions to identical economic problems with suboptimal solutions being among a larger set of solutions. A random shock to an economic system, be it large or small, will have a determining impact on which equilibrium solution becomes the dominant one, where the dominant solution can be the suboptimal one. Whichever solution is, in effect, chosen by the random event, this solution might be locked-in or become a permanent or a stable equilibrium... For this reason, one cannot expect the free market to force the economy to converge to unique equilibrium solutions to economic problems... More specifically, one cannot predict that the eventual stable equilib-rium solution will be the optimal one, even under conditions of competitive markets.

Even if comparative statics could locate the multiple equilibria associated with problems characterized by increasing returns and path dependency, Arthur (1989) argued, it is most unlikely that it could predict which one will actually occur. This is because 'insignificant circumstances become magnified by positive feedbacks to "tip" the system into the actual outcome "selected". The small events of history become important' (ibid, p127). He argued accordingly that economic problems featuring increasing returns are analysed more accurately as complex adaptive systems than as mechanistic systems.

A complex adaptive system consists of multiple autonomous elements in ongoing interaction with one another and with the system itself (Camazine et al, 2001). Arthur (1989, p107) discussed how the elements of this kind of system 'adapt to the world – the aggregate pattern – they co-create... As the elements react, the aggregate changes; as the aggregate changes, elements react anew'. Such a system is called complex not because it comprises a large number of elements but because its patterns of behaviour cannot be understood by focusing only on its elements. There is an emerging consensus that this kind of complexity is characteristic of environmental policy settings, or 'social-ecological systems',[1] where endogenously-organized social subsystems (e.g. common property arrangements) play key roles (Berkes et al, 2003; Anderies et al, 2004).

In contrast to a mechanistic system with unchanging relationships between unchanging parts, therefore, the parts of a complex adaptive system and the relationships between them are continually adapting to one another. The increasing returns driving this process amplify random events (e.g. chance meetings, emergence of leadership, elections, serendipitous inventions, unintended rule infractions) and can thereby flip a system into one of many possible paths. The timing of such a flip and its effect on the path taken are rarely predictable (Berkes, 2002).

In considering how economists should respond to the analytical challenge presented by complex adaptive systems, Arthur (1994, pp406–407) noted that humans faced with complex problems:

> look for patterns; and we simplify the problem by using these patterns to construct temporary hypotheses to work with. We carry out localized deductions based on our current hypotheses and act on them. As feedback from the environment comes in, we may strengthen or weaken our beliefs in our current hypotheses, discarding some when they cease to perform, and replacing them as needed with new ones ... Such behavior is inductive.

This observation is consistent with the growing consensus more generally that adaptive management is the most appropriate methodological response to environmental policy problems associated with complex adaptive systems – including the long-term challenge of pursuing sustainable development through collaborative environmental management. It accepts that problems of this kind can only be understood in the process of trying to solve them, and accordingly that it is implausible to expect that optimal institutional solutions can be identified at the outset. It recognizes that complex adaptive systems often evolve in surprising ways, including in response to manipulation of the system elements with which institutional choices are concerned. Dovers (1999a, p3) identified the standard response of policy makers to such surprises, at least in Australian environmental management, as one of muddling through on the basis of 'ad hocery and amnesia'. In contrast, adaptive management of any problem involves a systematic inductive process of: identifying patterns in prior institutional experiences; deriving hypotheses from these patterns to be tested in the problem at hand by appropriate institutional 'experiments'; identifying patterns in the outcomes of those experiments; updating prior hypotheses on the basis of these new patterns and choosing the next generation of institutional experiments accordingly; and so on.

Proponents of adaptive management recognize that the choice between institutional options for a given problem should not be determined solely by their immediate contributions to solving the problem but also by the opportunities they offer to learn about the problem. As Walters (1986, p257) observed in the context of fisheries management, institutional choices in adaptive management often involve trade-offs between these values: '[A]ctions that perturb the system state and output in an informative manner may require giving up immediate harvests'. Hence, adaptive management is not at all equivalent to rational-comprehensive planning with a renewed emphasis on monitoring and evaluation. Rational-comprehensive planning presumes that the problem at hand can be understood fully, and institutional solutions can be identified optimally, at the outset. Hence, followers of this approach – unlike practitioners of adaptive management – have no reason to experiment with institutional choices to test the bounds of the problem, or to monitor and evaluate outcomes of current institutional choices closely enough to justify more than incremental changes to those choices.

Complexity and adaptive management: A role for economics?

This convergence between the ideas of complexity economists and proponents of adaptive management suggests a way forward. It may help to fulfil the promise that the comparative institutions approach holds for increasing the sophistication and accuracy of economic analyses concerned with institutional choices in the kinds of complex environmental problems assigned increasingly to collaborative management approaches. A useful start in this direction is North's (1990) economic framework for historical analysis of institutional change, as informed by insights from complexity economics. This framework emerged from his dissatisfaction with the neoclassical theory of institutional evolution that grew out of Alchian's (1950) arguments regarding competitive selection and efficiency.

According to the neoclassical theory of institutional evolution – the classic reference for which is Demsetz (1967) – new institutions are adopted only when the benefits gained exceed the costs incurred. Institutional innovation thereby ensures maintenance of Pareto efficiency in the face of random events including development of new technologies, emergence of resource scarcities, and changes in individuals' preferences. As North (1990, p92) observed, the theory implies that 'over time inefficient institutions are weeded out, efficient ones survive, and thus there is a gradual evolution of more efficient forms of economic, political, and social organization'. If the theory were valid, he predicted, the performance of different national economies would converge over time as the inefficient institutional arrangements holding some nations back were replaced by efficient ones as a result of international competitive pressures. As he observed, however, 'the gap between rich and poor nations, between developed and undeveloped nations, is as wide today as it ever was and perhaps a great deal wider than ever before' (ibid, p6).

North recognized that the inaccuracy of the neoclassical prediction in this case derives from its failure to account for increasing returns. He explained that dynamics of this kind arise in the course of institutional change due to the internal and external economies unleashed by the change. The internal economies arise because '[t]he kinds of knowledge, skills, and learning that the members of an organization will acquire will reflect the payoff – the incentives – imbedded in the institutional constraints' (ibid, p74). In turn, '[t]he way in which knowledge develops influences the perceptions people have about the world around them and hence the way they rationalize, explain, and justify that world' (ibid, p76). Hence, any institutional change influences the path along which mental models and ideologies will evolve over time. In turn, the resulting mental models and ideologies will influence 'the perceptions of the entrepreneurs in political and economic organizations that they could do better by altering the existing institutional framework at some margin' (ibid, p8). In this way, the direction that institutional change takes at one juncture generates internal economies that affect subsequent rounds of institutional choices.

The external economies associated with an institutional change arise from network externalities emerging as a consequence of organizations adapting themselves to the incentives introduced by the change, and thus acquiring an interest in preserving the new institutions – including by attempting to influence the polity towards this end. As Dixit (1996, p26) has observed, '[p]olicy acts shape the future environment by creating constituencies that gain from the policy, who will then fiercely resist any changes that take away these gains'.

As a result of the combined effects of internal and external economies, institutional choices are normally path dependent. After a particular institutional option is selected, in other words, it becomes more costly to revert to an alternative option than it would have been to adopt that alternative in the first place. Path dependency thereby reduces institutional adaptability. This is not to suggest that the path dependency implications of all institutional options are likely to be similar. It is often the case that some options (e.g. those whose performance is more easily evaluated or which avoid creating cohesive constituencies with strong vested interests in maintaining those options) lead to less path dependency than others and thereby leave more scope subsequently for institutional adaptability.

Loss of institutional adaptability would be no cause for concern if confidence were warranted that institutional choices will be made optimally at the outset. Given the complexity of most such choices, however, such confidence is usually misplaced. Any institutional option chosen initially is typically revealed as suboptimal once actual events unfold. Consequently, North urged economists to account explicitly in their analyses of current institutional choices for the repercussions of these choices for future institutional adaptability. He proposed that this occur through adopting 'adaptive efficiency' as their choice criterion. Consistent with the focus of adaptive management, he defined this kind of efficiency as 'concerned with the willingness of a society to acquire knowledge and learning, to induce innovation, to undertake risk and creative activity of all sorts, as well as to resolve problems and bottlenecks of the society through time' (North, 1990, p80). Taking his lead from Alchian's (1950) evolutionary theory of economics, he reasoned that:

> The society that permits the maximum number of trials will be most likely to solve problems through time... Adaptive efficiency, therefore, provides the incentives to encourage the development of decentralized decision making processes that allow societies to maximize the efforts required to explore alternative ways of solving problems (North, 1990, p81).

Departing from Alchian's script, however, North recognized that path dependency of complex institutional choices means that maximizing competitive selection among institutional solutions is not sufficient to guarantee that lock in to a suboptimal path of institutional choices will be avoided. He emphasized consequently that:

> We must also learn from failures… There is nothing simple about this process, because organizational errors may be not only probabilistic, but also systematic, due to ideologies that may give people preferences for the kinds of solutions that are not oriented to adaptive efficiency (North, 1990, pp80–81).

Aside from increasing the number of institutional trials for a particular kind of social problem, Frey and Eichenberger (1999, p16) identified five further ways whereby decentralization of institutional choices can increase institutional adaptability:

> First, it is more likely that a majority of the population of one of the many small jurisdictions favours a certain innovation than the population of the whole country. Second, innovations under decentralization can be undertaken on an experimental basis within those jurisdictions where the conditions for success are most conducive and where the respective innovations are most desired. Third, voluntary experiments have higher success rates than when imposed from above. Fourth, a particular local jurisdiction finds it less risky to introduce new ideas … because the consequences are limited and can be controlled and influenced more easily. If the innovation proves a failure, not much is lost. Fifth, a successful innovation, on the other hand, will soon be imitated by other local units and will thus diffuse over the whole country.

Decentralization also increases societal capacity to learn from these trials, because it means that 'individuals who have the greatest interest in overcoming [commons problems] learn the results of the experimentation with rules and can adapt to this direct feedback' (Ostrom, 1999, p525). In contrast, centralized approaches to institutional decision making impede inductive learning in complex settings since they 'obscure through aggregation and averaging… the patterns… of the system' (Wilson, 2002, p345).

Gains in adaptive efficiency can also arise from decentralization allowing a better fit, compared with centralized decision making, between the group of people affected by a decision and the group of people with rights to participate in that decision. Ostrom et al (1999b, p37) called these groups, respectively, the 'public' and the 'political community' for a particular decision. Where the political community associated with centralized decision making is broader than the associated public, this can lead, as explained below, to decisions ill-adapted to the interests of the relevant public:

> [W]here the political community contains the whole public

and, in addition, people unaffected by a transaction, the unaffected are given a voice when none may be desired. Capricious actions can result. The total political community in a city of three million population may not be an appropriate decision-making mechanism in planning a local playground (ibid, p37).

A further important advantage of decentralization for adaptive efficiency is that it strengthens the political selective pressures at work on institutional choices. As observed by Frey and Eichenberger (1999, pp3, 31):

> Elections . . . are not able to sufficiently restrict politicians' selfish behaviour. Therefore, institutional conditions have to be designed so that stronger incentives are imposed on politicians and governments to fulfill citizens' preferences. This can only be achieved by strengthening the political competition at all levels . . . [Organizational units decentralized policy functions] are subject to comparison and competition with other jurisdictions. The central state, in contrast, assumes a monopolistic position with respect to its inhabitants . . . This privileged position makes it profitable for rent-seeking activities by organized pressure groups. The interests of [the general citizenry] and other weakly organized groups tend to be neglected in this rent-seeking struggle.

Nevertheless, there are normally limits to what can be achieved by complete decentralization. For instance, local groups decentralized such responsibilities may not be able to discharge them without imposing externalities on other local groups and thereby creating inter-group conflicts that such groups cannot resolve by their own devices. Such groups may also find it difficult to resolve longstanding conflicts within their membership, enforce the choices they make, or raise the resources required to understand the problem and develop solutions. Ostrom (1999) argued that the way to address these limitations while maintaining adaptive capacity is through the kinds of nested systems of organization that were identified in the previous chapter as a key to solving large-group problems of collective action.

Through nested systems, citizens can retain many of the advantages of a fully decentralized system, including the ability to use their local knowledge in developing rules, and to gain relatively direct feedback regarding how the rules introduced are performing. Furthermore, 'problems associated with local tyrannies and inappropriate discrimination can be addressed in larger, general-purpose governmental units that are responsible for protecting the rights for all citizens and the oversight of appropriate exercises of authority within smaller units of government' (ibid, p528). The overlapping of governance in such multi-scale systems contributes to adaptive capacity in further ways. It can allow information about rules that have worked for one unit to be transmitted more easily to other units. Another key advantage of this overlapping is that 'when small systems fail, there are larger systems to call upon – and vice versa' (ibid, p528).

The advantages for adaptive efficiency of pursuing large-group collective action through nested systems are typically invisible for those trained to view the world through a Progressive mindset. Ostrom et al (1999b, p31) observed accordingly that the common view regards a 'multiplicity of political units ... [as] essentially a pathological phenomenon' and as 'too many governments and not enough government'. Frey and Eichenberger (1999, p214, original emphasis) considered a Swiss case of polycentric governance regarded by the relevant authorities as inefficient and found that 'this "inefficiency" refers at best to administrative cost, but *in particular* does not take into account the benefits by supplying more closely to the citizens' preferences, and neglects the better adjustment to changing circumstances of the future'.

A comparative institutions framework for adaptive environmental management

The insight that collective action in solving complex problems is best pursued through nested systems – including collaborative systems – may be important, but institutional design of such systems in particular settings is itself complex (Ostrom, 1999). What potential is there for economic analysis to help with the learning needed for adaptive management to incrementally uncover solutions to these design problems?

A Paretian approach to comparative analysis of complex institutional choices

The work of Challen (2000) suggests that economic analysis has indeed a significant contribution to make in this area. In this work, North's (1990) insights regarding the influence of past institutional choices on present choices were used as the basis of a framework for analysing the cost effectiveness of present institutional choices. In so far as this framework accounts for increasing returns and path dependency, it represents an important advance on how economists had previously applied the comparative institutions approach to analysis of present institutional choices. At the same time, however, it subscribes to the value judgements associated with the Paretian approach of mainstream economics to institutional analysis – that is, the value judgements underpinning the principle of individual sovereignty and the potential Pareto improvement criterion. Accordingly, its objective function deems the optimal institutional option given a particular choice to be the one that minimizes the sum of the costs incurred by all individuals, measured in monetary units, in the process of achieving a given policy target (e.g. a water quality standard).

Challen assumed implicitly that the only costs affected by institutional choices are transaction costs, but he distinguished 'dynamic' and 'static' transaction costs. He defined dynamic transaction costs as the costs incurred in effecting institutional change, and static transaction costs as the costs of decision making within a given institutional structure. He also distinguished two types of dynamic transaction costs. The first of these comprises the 'institutional transition costs' into the future of deciding upon and implementing an institutional change in the current period.[2] These costs arise as a function of the existing institutional structure. He included within institutional transition costs the costs incurred due to the following aspects of institutional change:

- research and institutional design;
- negotiation, bargaining and decision making;
- political repercussions to decision makers;
- institutional creation, including the drafting of legislation, policies, etc.;
- implementation, including associated education activities;
- obsolescence of investments in existing institutional structures;
- social displacement of individuals and firms affected by institutional change;
- compensation payments to parties disadvantaged by institutional change;
- costs associated with lobbying by interest groups;
- increased perceptions of sovereign risk and policy uncertainty.

Challen's second type of dynamic transaction costs, 'institutional lock-in costs', arise from recognizing that current institutional choices, to the extent that they generate future path dependencies, increase the transition costs of possible future institutional changes. His primary concern in highlighting this category of costs was on the negative implications that decentralization of property rights can have, via the network externalities it unleashes, for future institutional adaptability. He explained this concern as follows:

> Generally speaking, the political ramifications of institutional change are greater if the costs and/or benefits of change are incurred by small and/or concentrated groups in society that are able to mobilize resources for political lobbying, as opposed to large and/or dispersed groups. Consequently, it is relatively easy (low cost) for political decisions to be made that transfer property rights from a large dispersed group to a small concentrated group, but relatively difficult (high cost) to make the reverse change. Hence the notion of irreversibility of institutional change.
>
> A generalization can be made to the case of institutional change within a hierarchical model of institutions for regulation of natural resources. For the most part, property rights at lower levels of an institutional hierarchy tend to be concentrated into smaller societal groups than at higher levels in the hierarchy... As a general rule it would be relatively easy (low political costs) to transfer property rights down such an institutional hierarchy, but difficult (high political costs) to transfer property rights back up the hierarchy (Challen, 2000, p178).

As a result of focusing exclusively on institutional choices relating to how far property rights should be decentralized, and of looking only within this focus at the relationship between decentralization and the power of vested interests, Challen presumed that the institutional lock-in costs of all institutional options are positive, albeit in varying degrees. As the earlier discussion made clear, however, decentralization of property rights can also, through increasing opportunities for experimenting with institutional options and learning from the experiences gained thereby, have positive implications for future institutional adaptability. The ultimate effect of decentralizing property rights on institutional lock-in costs in a particular setting will depend, therefore, on how the positive and negative implications weigh up against one another in that setting. In so far as the net effect of a decentralization option in a setting is to increase future institutional adaptability, then the institutional lock-in costs of the option take a negative value.

Moreover, institutional choices are not concerned exclusively with the degree to which property rights should be decentralized. They are concerned with a vast range of other issues like deciding when a group has reached agreement (e.g. majority vote or consensus), setting conditions of group membership, selecting office holders, hiring and promoting staff, punishing free riders, rewarding cooperators, organizing public participation, adjudicating conflicts, maintaining financial accountability, and so on. Even though Challen's focus did not extend beyond the decentralization issue, his framework is general enough to apply to all kinds of institutional choices. Of particular relevance to this book is its ability to account for differences in how specific institutional options influence future institutional adaptability within a setting by affecting stocks of trust and social capital more generally (e.g. social norms and leadership). Consider a case where the institutional option chosen by an organizational unit representing a group's interests serves to strengthen 'horizontal' trust among its members (e.g. by providing increased incentives for the social interaction they need to monitor one another's trustworthiness and informally sanction any breaches of trust detected), such that the ongoing capacity of the members to fulfil their collective interests through voluntary cooperation is strengthened. This increase in trust will tend to reduce the costs of ongoing institutional adaptability in pursuit of those interests (i.e. institutional lock-in costs), all else remaining equal. To the extent that the option chosen serves to reduce trust among group members (e.g. by reducing the incentives for them to interact socially or by setting them at odds with one another), conversely, institutional lock-in costs will be greater than otherwise, all else remaining equal.

A further trust-related issue relevant for institutional lock-in costs is the effect of the institutional option chosen by an organizational unit representing a group's interests on the 'vertical' trust invested in that unit by group members. To the extent that the institutional option chosen makes the organizational unit more trusted by group members (e.g. because the option supports or 'nests' their own efforts to fulfil their collective needs rather than, as they had previously come to expect, frustrates them), we can expect the institutional adaptability of that system to be increased, all else remaining equal (i.e. to the extent that their increased trust in the organizational unit makes group members more likely to accept its next round of institutional choices).

The institutional lock-in costs of such a trust-building option will therefore tend to be reduced, all else remaining equal. Where, in contrast, the institutional option chosen makes the organizational unit responsible for the choice less trusted by group members (e.g. by conflicting with members' social norms to a greater degree than they had previously come to expect), the institutional adaptability of the system is likely to be reduced. The institutional lock-in costs of such a trust-eroding option will accordingly be increased, all else remaining equal.

As explained by Challen, positive institutional lock-in costs represent a loss of quasi-option value. This type of value derives from the information gained by not making a choice now but spending more time to learn about its consequences. Such value is forfeited to the extent that an institutional choice made now, through increasing future institutional transition costs, reduces subsequent possibilities for institutional experimentation and thereby reduces opportunities available for learning how to adapt towards the optimal path of institutional choices. Conversely, negative institutional lock-in costs equate to a gain of quasi-option value.

Following from this typology of transaction costs, Challen proposed that the optimal institutional choice is that which minimizes the sum of static transaction costs, institutional transition costs and institutional lock-in costs incurred in achieving a given policy target. However, this cost effectiveness criterion fails to account for all types of costs potentially affected by an institutional choice. Institutional choices typically influence 'transformation costs' as well as transaction costs. Transformation costs, otherwise known as 'production costs', are the costs of providing a good in a world of zero transaction costs. It is quite possible for the transaction cost advantages of an institutional option to be outweighed by transformation cost disadvantages (McCann et al, 2005). Challen's framework needs to be extended, therefore, to account for the effects of the different options on transformation costs as well as on transaction costs. As with transaction costs, static and dynamic types of transformation costs can be distinguished. Static transformation costs are the costs of operating a given technology under a given institutional structure. Dynamic transformation costs are the costs arising from the influence of a given institutional change on individuals' choices of technologies.

As with transaction costs, two types of dynamic transformation costs can be distinguished. 'Technological transition costs' are those costs incurred due to the influence of a particular current institutional choice on individuals' current choices of technologies. 'Technological lock-in costs' arise to the extent that technological choices arising from a current institutional change create path dependencies in technology adoption. Such path dependencies create constituencies committed to resisting any reversal of the current institutional change that led to this path of technological choices. In turn, the creation of such constituencies increases the costs of reversing a current institutional choice. Consider the case of an institutional change permitting the commercial harvesting of fish within a zone that was previously closed to such activity, such that substantial new investments in commercial fishing capacity occur. It would hardly be surprising if subsequent efforts to reverse the institutional change met staunch political opposition from the fishers who invested in increasing their harvesting capacity. As with institutional lock-in costs, technological lock-in costs can also be equated with a loss of quasi-option value. They reduce the rate of future technological and institutional experimentation and thus the accumulation of information useful in guiding adaptation towards superior technologies and institutional structures.

When these additional cost considerations are accounted for in Challen's framework, the Paretian cost effectiveness criterion for institutional choice becomes one of identifying the institutional option that minimizes the sum of all the costs incurred within the following six categories, measured in monetary terms (and discounted appropriately to the extent that they occur in the future), in the process of achieving a given policy target:

- static transaction costs;
- institutional transition costs;
- institutional lock-in costs;
- static transformation costs;
- technological transition costs;
- technological lock-in costs.

Despite the conceptual advance represented by this criterion, its empirical application to an actual institutional choice faced in the present entails a real challenge. It involves predicting the effects of each institutional option in terms of each of the six cost categories accounted for in the measure. Prediction will normally be easiest for static transformation costs and technological transition costs. Indeed, cost effectiveness analysis by environmental economists has conventionally been limited to consideration of these costs.

The task of predicting static transaction costs and institutional transition costs is likely to be considerably more difficult. Challen (2000, p207) remarked that rigorous practical application of his framework 'is impeded by a lack of techniques and methodology for *ex ante* estimation of transaction costs'. He attributed the problem of predicting static transaction costs and institutional transition costs to 'their diversity, uncertain functional relationships between the costs and their determinants, many costs being implicit or indirect, and many costs not being easily quantified in dollar terms' (ibid, p192). Nevertheless, significant progress has been made in developing typologies of transaction costs (Thompson, 1999; McCann et al, 2005) that offer at least a coherent structure for ex ante estimation of these types of transaction costs. Moreover, it may be possible to estimate some categories of transaction costs by adapting techniques developed for non-market valuation of environmental goods, including the contingent valuation method and choice modelling (McCann et al, 2005).

The problems faced in predicting technological and institutional transition costs will arise also in predicting technological and institutional lock-in costs, respectively, since the lock-in costs comprise future effects on transition costs. In addition, the path dependencies responsible for institutional lock-in costs mean that these costs cannot be predicted credibly by the method of comparative statics (which, as explained earlier, cannot account for the increasing returns responsible for path dependencies). The same applies for technological lock-in costs. Since techniques for non-market valuation like contingent valuation and choice modelling are based on the method of comparative statics – which assumes there is a single equilibrium value to be estimated – their use in predicting costs in these two categories is also not credible.

If technological lock-in costs and institutional lock-in costs cannot be predicted through comparative statics, does this mean that the cost effectiveness framework presented here is of no use to economists in accounting empirically for the consequences of path dependencies for the cost effectiveness of institutional options? No, it does not, but it does mean that economists need to look beyond comparative statics when they come to predict these costs, and use instead the kind of inductive method proposed by Arthur (1994). A strategy for doing so is outlined in Chapter 7. Challen (2000, p203) seemed to acknowledge the advantages of applying his framework through an inductive method when he proposed that future empirical research within his framework use the results of past studies of particular institutional arrangements to construct general models that allow prediction of the transaction costs that may be incurred under such arrangements in other specific social-ecological settings. Even without full empirical application of the framework, he argued that the framework is useful since it:

> provide[s] a framework for many existing *ad hoc* approaches to policy analysis and offers direction to future research aimed at more rigorous comparative studies of institutions within contexts of history and of imperfect information on economic outcomes of institutional change.

It may be instructive at this point to clarify how the approach to economic analysis of institutional choices described above differs from an approach that has become embraced rapidly by mainstream economists. This mainstream approach derives from the new institutional economics (NIE), or more particularly – given that the NIE remains 'a boiling cauldron of ideas' (Williamson, 2000, p610) – from that dominant school of the NIE taking its lead from the work of Oliver Williamson (1975; 1985; 1996; 2000). Williamson followed Coase's (1937; 1960) lead in extending neoclassical economics beyond an analysis of market (i.e. production and consumption) choices to institutional (including contractual) choices. This strand of the NIE shares much in common with transaction cost economics (Williamson, 2000).

The Williamson school of the NIE (WNIE) has certainly contributed to the sophistication with which mainstream economists now analyse institutional choices. Due to its influence, they are now more likely to consider the implications of transaction costs for their analyses. The NIE has also made a valuable contribution by highlighting to mainstream economists the need when designing current institutional arrangements to anticipate the need to adapt those arrangements as the future unfolds.

At first glance, indeed, the WNIE seems in tune with the approach to economic analysis of institutional choices outlined above. Members of this school purport to acknowledge that economic actors are boundedly rational when faced with complex institutional choices. Accordingly, they have discarded the presumption in the agency theoretic tradition of institutional economics that optimal institutional arrangements can be designed once-and-for-all at the outset (i.e. without the need for the arrangements to be adapted as the future unfolds). Consequently, they focus predominantly on the ex post stage of institutional design (i.e. after the initial design choice is made). Williamson (2000, p599) explained that this shift followed from recognition that 'adaptation is the central problem of economic organization'.

All said and done, however, the WNIE redefines bounded rationality and the problem of institutional adaptation such that path dependency of institutional choices is effectively ignored.[3] Williamson (1996, p239) has acknowledged that his analytical method remains one of 'comparative statics – which is a once-for-all exercise'. As highlighted by Slater and Spencer (2000), he addressed the inconsistency of bounded rationality with comparative statics by introducing 'farsightedness' as a supplementary aspect of rationality. This farsightedness provides individuals with 'the capacities to learn and look ahead, perceive hazards, and factor these back into the contractual relation, thereafter to devise responsive institutions' (Williamson, 1996, p71). It enables individuals to perfectly anticipate, and plan contingencies for, all the consequences of their bounded rationality when making their once-and-for-all institutional choices. These choices include prescriptions for how any institutional design implemented at the outset is to be adapted as future events unfold. Farsightedness ensures these events can be predicted perfectly, so that adaptations to them can be decided optimally at the outset. As Slater and Spencer (2000, p71) emphasized, the introduction of farsightedness to the WNIE analytical framework rendered bounded rationality effectively meaningless:

> Clearly, it makes little sense to speak of people suffering from bounded rationality when they simultaneously retain the capacity for farsightedness, allowing them to foresee a way round the problems of complexity and uncertainty at the outset of contracting.

Unlike in the economic approach to institutional analysis developed above, therefore, the WNIE does not admit the possibility of suboptimal institutional choices and thus the need for adaptive management. Given farsightedness, there is never a need for economic actors to reverse their institutional choices, and thus never a reason to factor into their choices the costs associated with any path dependencies the choices create. Farsightedness also removes any reason to factor into choices any differences between options in the opportunities for experimentation and learning they would generate. Indeed, it means that there is no institutional choice, or set of institutional choices, challenging enough that it cannot be solved by a centralized decision making system optimally at the outset. Ultimately, therefore, the WNIE denies the need not only for adaptive management but also for collaborative environmental management. This explains why mainstream economists typically reduce the meaning of collaboration to a process where problems are defined and solved centrally and implementation of solutions is 'contracted out' or 'outsourced' (e.g. through schemes offering grants to local groups prepared to undertake environmental projects consistent with a centrally sponsored strategy) only in order to reduce implementation costs.

A political economy approach to comparative analysis of complex institutional choices

The cost effectiveness framework outlined above offers a more sophisticated conceptual basis for economic analysis of complex, path-dependent institutional choices than has been available previously. Nevertheless, it remains restrictive as a vehicle for analysing institutional choices in pursuit of the collaborative vision for environmental management. Proponents of this vision see collaboration among different stakeholders as a process of deliberative discourse which helps to dissolve inter-stakeholder conflict by moving them, as boundedly rational actors, towards consensus on knowledge and value systems they can use to better reach agreement on their shared problem and on how alternative institutional solutions to that problem should be ranked (Wondolleck and Yaffee, 2000; Innes and Booher, 2003; Bryan, 2004). Deliberative discourse relies on 'establishing conditions of free public reasoning among equals who are governed by the decisions' (Cohen, 1998, p186). Such conditions can allow an atmosphere of mutual trust to emerge within which:

> on the one hand, people (and collectivities) may come to abandon or relinquish priorly held perceptions and claims . . . ; and, on the other hand, they may accede to new perceptions, convictions and motivations . . . It is precisely the fluid, unfinished, ambiguous process of inter-subjective communication . . . that permits the emergence of novel perspectives of coexistence and compromise (O'Connor, 2000, p5).

As we have seen previously, mainstream economics is ideologically opposed to any process, deliberative or not, that seeks to change individuals' values or preferences. As explained in Chapter 1, Arrow's Impossibility Theorem was widely interpreted within economics as demonstrating that a stable, unique preference ranking for a group cannot be derived from the preference rankings of its members without retreating from classical liberalism's commitment to protecting individuals' rights of privacy. The theorem suggests, also, that a value system for a group decided by its members is inevitably influenced by how the decision process is organized, and that any such process is therefore susceptible to strategic manipulation (Arrow and Raynaud, 1986). Hence, mainstream economists continue to regard any effort within a group to reach agreement on a common preference ranking as necessarily paternalistic and undemocratic, and to advocate instead that any preference ranking for a group be derived technically; that is through a Paretian approach founded on the value judgements underpinning the potential Pareto improvement criterion and the principle of individual sovereignty.

Notwithstanding the stance of mainstream economics, a robust tradition has persisted among leading economists across the wider profession, wherein changes in individuals' preferences arising from deliberative discussion and disputation are not regarded as paternalistic but as essential for effective democracy. Hence, Buchanan (1954, p120) remarked that 'the definition of democracy as "government by discussion" implies that individual values can and do change in the process of decision-making'. Sen (1995, p18) found 'Buchanan is right to emphasize the role of public discussion in the development of preferences (as an important part of democracy)'. Knight (1947, p280) observed along similar lines that 'values are established or validated and recognized through discussion, an activity which is at once social, intellectual and creative'. Indeed, Boulding (1970, p118) regarded the idea that individuals' preferences should be quarantined from disputation as 'absurd'.

Economists critical of the principle of individual sovereignty emphasize how the preferences held by individuals can diverge considerably from their best interests. The likelihood of such a divergence in contemporary times has been highlighted powerfully by Norgaard (1994), by means of the co-evolutionary framework he introduced to economics. This framework portrays development as a process of co-evolution between five subsystems: knowledge, values, organization, technology, and the natural environment. Random changes, chance discoveries and deliberate innovations occur in each subsystem which influence, by modifying selection pressures, the qualities and distribution of components in each of the other subsystems. Consequently, the subsystems co-evolve such that each reflects the other.

We saw in Chapter 1 how modernist beliefs – of objectivism (including materialism), universalism, mechanism, atomism (including individualism) and monism – became entrenched in human knowledge systems around the world as a result of facilitating the scientific and technological breakthroughs responsible for the scientific and industrial revolutions. The resulting shift in knowledge systems brought about far-reaching changes in the selection pressures shaping the evolution of value systems. Accordingly, for instance, selection pressures came to favour those individuals more interested in materialistic outcomes and more inclined towards individualistic and mechanistic ways of operating. Norgaard (ibid) explained how access to stocks of fossil hydrocarbons freed industrialized societies for many years from a wide range of selection pressures that the natural environment would otherwise have exerted on modernist beliefs and values. Even though major problems (e.g. social dislocation and pollution) did arise as a result of societies coming to co-evolve around combustion of fossil fuels rather than in accordance with selection pressures exerted by their natural environments, there was fairly general confidence – at least in those nations that modernized most success-fully – that these problems were more than compensated by the advantages modernization continued to deliver.

This confidence has of course turned around somewhat since the 1970s. The sustainable development concept to which many governments around the world committed themselves reflects this loss of confidence. It emphasizes also the need for beliefs and values to change in significant ways so that the choices made in satisfying the needs of present generations do not compromise the ability of future generations to satisfy theirs. To date, however, the search for solutions to the problems of modernization remains largely guided by modernist beliefs and the values that co-evolved with them. For instance, mainstream economists continue to argue influentially that market-oriented institutional arrangements are capable by themselves of delivering sustainable development, the implication being that efforts to adapt individual and collective values are unwarranted.

In contrast, Sen (1995, p18) argued that '[m]any of the more exacting problems of the contemporary world – varying from famine prevention to environmental preservation – actually call for value formation through public discussion'. He recognized that conflicts between the values or preference rankings that different individuals bring to a complex problem often follow in significant part from the difficulty of understanding the problem. Individuals obtain feedback through public deliberation that can help to correct their misunderstandings and thereby narrow differences in their preference rankings. Adaptation of individuals' preferences through public deliberation can thereby make it possible in contentious problems to shift from the 'lowest common denominator' options to which institutional reform efforts are often restricted when existing preference rankings are taken as given, to the more far-reaching options typically needed to solve such problems. Accordingly, Randall (1999, p32) observed within the environmental policy arena that '[s]tructured discourse and deliberation can often undermine conflict, and careful consideration of information can erode firmly held priors and open up new possibilities'.

Norton et al (1998, p200) referred to such deliberation as 'democratic preference change'. They characterized it as involving 'rational suasion, of pointing out to people the consequences of their desires, and showing them alternative paths to personal satisfaction that have less severe impacts on the future of society'. It is inappropriate to regard such suasion as paternalistic, they argued, if it follows rules decided democratically. After all, as Boulding (1970) pointed out, we spend much of our lives disputing over preferences, and mostly this does not involve paternalism but rather a mutually respectful exchange of opinions. Arguments are usually resolved with civility, even if not everyone is completely satisfied with the result.

In any case, as Norton et al (1998) observed, it is now commonplace that individuals are beset from all sides by attempts to change their preferences. Often the parties making these attempts are driven more by their own interests than those of the people whose preferences they seek to change. And often the attempts (e.g. via public relations campaigns) involve manipulation more than rational suasion. Processes of democratic preference change can therefore offer individuals opportunities to resist the preference-changing agendas of vested interests and thereby gain greater sovereignty over their preference choices than they could achieve independently. As these authors asked rhetorically, is it 'better for preferences to be determined behind the scenes... [o]r do we want to explore and shape them openly, based on social dialogue and consensus, with a higher goal in mind?' (ibid, p196).

Hence, the view that collaborative environmental management as a deliberative decision making process has an important role to play in lessening conflicts over institutional choices is not without significant sympathy from economists outside the mainstream of their profession. Moreover, an approach to economic analysis of institutional choices suited to supporting such a deliberative process has already been conceptualized by Schmid (1989) – the 'political economy approach' to cost–benefit analysis and cost effectiveness analysis. In this approach, the proper role for cost–benefit analysis in a democratic society is as:

> a framework for systematically displaying the consequences of alternative [institutional options] in such a manner that the ranking of these alternatives is the result of applying *politically chosen* rules reflecting explicit performance objectives (ibid, p285, emphasis added).

It follows that cost–benefit analysis is seen in this approach as:

> a dialogue between analyst and public decision makers. It is not something the analyst does alone and presents finished to the world... Decision makers are not always ready to answer the questions put to them by analysts. In many cases their objectives have not been thought out... [Hence, the role of the independent analyst is to] raise the necessary questions requiring political resolution of conflicting interests and stimulate a range of likely answers (ibid, p286).

The solution, therefore, to the restrictiveness of the cost effectiveness framework presented above, at least as a tool for analysing institutional choices in pursuit of the collaborative vision, is to replace the Paretian approach it applies in identifying a collective preference ranking with a political economy approach. The objective function after such a modification still entails minimization of the total costs incurred in achieving a policy target. The differences are that: (a) the total costs would be measured for each choice in accordance with a collective preference ranking agreed upon by the relevant political community (e.g. one that weights costs incurred by members of poorer groups more heavily than costs incurred by wealthier groups), rather than on a preference ranking derived technically using the Paretian approach; and (b) the policy target and collective preference ranking may evolve over a number of iterative interactions between the analyst and the political community's representatives. Challen (2000, p203) commented himself on the restrictiveness of the Paretian approach upon which he founded his economic framework for analysis of institutional choices, noting that a shortcoming of his framework was that 'effects on the distribution of transaction costs have been ignored'.

Barriers to adoption

An approach to economic analysis capable of engaging credibly with the complexity of institutional choices entailed in pursuing the collaborative vision for environmental management was developed in this chapter. Nevertheless, application of this framework presents a significant challenge for economists. The problem that mainstream economists concerned with ex ante institutional analysis normally highlight – that of measuring transaction costs within a comparative statics framework – constitutes only a small part of the challenge presented by the approach developed here. The larger part of this challenge involves predicting the costs arising from institutional choices as a result of path dependencies. These costs cannot be explained or predicted using the method of comparative statics to which mainstream economics has become ideologically committed. Detaching from this commitment in order to account for costs associated with institutional path dependency will likely be the hardest part of the challenge for most economists to surmount.

It is necessary therefore to convince mainstream economists that the inability of comparative statics to account for costs associated with path dependency is serious enough to warrant augmenting it with another, inductive, method in order that such costs can be accounted for. This will not be easy given that, first, comparative statics yields the predictive precision that mainstream economics has sought to satisfy Progressive expectations of a scientific discipline and, second, an inductive method cannot yield such precision. Indeed, Williamson (2000, pp596, 604) has observed that prediction is the hallmark of a 'progressive research program', arguing that '[w]ould-be theories for which predictive content is lacking must eventually step aside (be set aside)'. He emphasized the importance of predictive capacity for the new institutional economics by answering Arrow's (1987, p737) question '[w]hy did the older institutionalist school [within economics] fail so miserably?' with the explanation that this failure resulted from the older school slipping into speculation rather than prediction. He distinguished speculation and prediction with the following words from Mitchell (1945, p2): 'Speculative systems... do not require the economist... to test hypotheses for conformity to fact, to discard those which do not fit, to invent new ones and test them until, at long last, he has established a factually valid theory'.

To be sure, speculation is no scientific basis for theory building. However, the deductive method of comparative statics is not the only one that economists can use to develop theory on the basis of prediction rather than speculation. Inductive methods capable of predicting complex economic phenomena more accurately, albeit less precisely, are also available. These ultimately need to be adopted if economists are to maintain their scientific credibility in analysing complex institutional choices. Nevertheless, a methodological shift of this significance cannot be expected to occur without evidence that inductive research methods can indeed contribute knowledge capable of improving institutional choices. The case study method has been a mainstay of efforts to date by social scientists, including some economists, to learn inductively from experiences in community-based and other collaborative approaches to environmental management. Accordingly, the aim in the next two chapters is to illustrate the potential of case study research to yield knowledge useful in realizing the collaborative vision more successfully than has occurred to date.

Part III

Lessons from the Field

Challenges and Strategies for Collaborative Environmental Management: Insights from International Experience

Policy makers and scholars interested in collaborative approaches to complex multi-scale problems of environmental management are coming increasingly to conceptualize such approaches as involving nested organizational systems. In such systems, decision making occurs relatively autonomously across multiple organizational subunits. Higher-level subunits nest lower-level ones, therefore, rather than centralize their functions. As highlighted in the previous chapter, this conceptualization of collaborative approaches to environmental management in terms of nested organizational systems coincides with a growing acceptance that such systems are understood most usefully as complex adaptive systems. Beyond this growing acceptance, however, efforts to establish nested organizational systems for environmental management remain handicapped by weak development of the relevant theory (Berkes, 2002).

The aim in this chapter is to help provide a foundation for theory building in this domain through adaptive management by bringing together a range of lessons gleaned from or prompted by international case studies of nested organizational approaches to environmental and natural resource management in rural areas. The chapter proceeds in the next section with a brief discussion of two core challenges faced in designing successful nested organizational systems for environmental management. Lessons of relevance to addressing each of these challenges are discussed in the subsequent two sections. The practical significance of these lessons is illustrated with evidence from particular cases. The chapter closes with a summary of the lessons identified for designing collaborative systems of environmental management as nested systems.

Two core challenges

Scholars interested in the management of complex multi-scale environmental issues have focused almost exclusively on the problem of allocating governance tasks across different levels of social organization. Young (2002a; 2002b) has suggested that this emphasis on allocation of tasks across organizational or institutional levels is too narrow, since it neglects what he called 'vertical interplay' or 'cross-scale interactions' between how tasks are performed at different levels. He observed that such interactions are common in the modern world, where the density of institutional arrangements operating in a given social space is normally high. Hence, he argued that:

> The extent to which specific environmental or resource regimes yield outcomes that are sustainable – much less efficient or equitable – is a function not only of the allocation of tasks between or among institutions operating at different levels of social organization but also of cross-scale interactions among distinct institutional arrangements (Young, 2002b, p266).

One of the cases Young (ibid) used to illustrate his argument was the sea tenure system in the eastern Bering Sea Region. Mostly in response to diminishing catches of salmon during the 1970s, the US state of Alaska established a limited entry regime for the inshore fisheries of the area. This state-scale initiative resulted in a number of unintended side effects, due in large part to unanticipated interactions with local-scale institutional arrangements. The limited entry system disrupted informal arrangements allowing a flexible mix of subsistence and commercial fishing. The price of permits to enter the fishery became such that young local people became less able to afford entry than had traditionally been the case. The marketability of permits caused further unexpected social upheaval in the local coastal community in so far as the financial insecurity of rural fishers led many of them to sell their permits to cope with short-term cash shortfalls, and thus to exit the fishery.

Accordingly, Young (ibid) urged those studying and designing institutional solutions to multi-scale environmental problems to extend their thinking beyond the problem of assigning tasks across organizational levels to the further problem of managing the cross-scale interactions that any assignment would generate. He proposed that the key to success in solving these two problems 'lies in allocating specific tasks to the appropriate level of social organization and then taking steps to ensure that the cross-scale interactions produce complementary rather than conflicting actions' (ibid, p266).

This proposal structures the search in the remainder of this chapter for lessons about how complex environmental problems might be solved more successfully through nested organizational systems. The discussion turns first to lessons concerned with allocating tasks across organizational levels, and then proceeds to consider lessons in respect of how cross-level complementarity in how tasks are conducted might best be ensured.

Core challenge 1: Matching tasks to levels

Subsidiarity

The focus of scholars and policy makers on the problem of allocating tasks across organizational levels has revolved largely around the 'principle of subsidiarity'. The original justification for this principle was moral, stemming from 'a conviction that each human individual is endowed with an inherent and inalienable worth, or dignity, and thus that the value of the individual is prior to the state or other social grouping' (British Institute of International and Comparative Law, 2003, p2). This conviction implied that a higher level of organization should refrain from undertaking tasks that could be performed just as well by a grouping closer to the individual. Pope Pius XI adopted this stance when, in Encyclical *Quadragesimo Anno* (1931), he formulated the subsidiarity principle as follows:

> It is an injustice and at the same time a great evil and disturbance of right order to assign to a greater and higher association what lesser and subordinate organisations can do. For every social activity ought of its very nature to furnish help to the members of the body social and never destroy and absorb them.

Aside from the moral justification, the subsidiarity principle is now also widely hypothesized to have practical advantages as a basis for social organization in response to multi-scale problems. Schumacher (1973) was instrumental in drawing public attention to these purported advantages when, in *Small is Beautiful*, he included the subsidiarity principle as a key principle for successful large-scale organization. The nations of Europe adopted this principle as one of the central constitutional principles for the European Union (made effective with the signing of the Amsterdam Treaty in 1999). A version of the principle appears as Principle 10 of the 1992 Rio Declaration on Environment and Development ('Issues are best handled with the participation of all concerned citizens, at the relevant level'). In 1993, the Board of the World Bank endorsed a *Water Resources Management Policy Paper* acknowledging the need to organize water resources management in accordance with this principle (World Bank, 1993). More recently, McKean (2002, p8) has proposed that the advantages of small groups in achieving voluntary cooperation can be extended to large-scale environmental problems by means of 'nested groups... with subsidiarity'. Connor and Dovers (2004, p72) commented along similar lines that '[s]ustainable development in a highly connected and complex world implies the necessary application of the subsidiarity principle, within a nested hierarchy of governance institutions'.

Despite widespread interest in and endorsement of the subsidiarity principle as a guide for organizing responses to such problems, consensus on the lowest organizational level at which a task can be performed effectively is typically not easy to come by. Robinson (1996, p10), the United Nations Commissioner for Human Rights during 1997–2002, remarked that 'the chief advantage of subsidiarity seems to be its capacity to mean all things to all interested parties – simultaneously'. Based on his study of decentralization rhetoric and reality in the context of Ghanaian forestry, deGrassi (2003, p1) concluded that '[s]ubsidiarity may raise more questions than it solves'. Nevertheless, Carozza (2003, p79) has argued as follows that concerns of this kind derive from unrealistic expectations:

> The detailed criteria by which subsidiarity operates are not suited

> to abstract reasoning *ex ante*, but instead need to be worked out
> over time, and the conclusions to which it leads will always be
> contextual and dynamic, containing the fluidity and flexibility
> of ... practical judgment.

At the very least, he observed, the principle provides stimulus for more thoughtful consideration about how, in any given context, different tasks should be allocated vertically within a system of social organization. At the same time as it challenges Progressive presumptions that all tasks of collective action should be centralized, it also highlights how decentralization of all tasks to local levels is normally too simplistic. In addition, he implied, the likelihood of the subsidiarity principle leading to a multiplicity of policy interpretations can be beneficial in terms of adaptive management – to the extent that learning is promoted by increased heterogeneity of policy choices.

This does not mean we are without guideposts in applying the subsidiarity principle to multi-scale environmental problems. There is much to learn from previous thought and action in this direction. Ribot (2002, p3) recommended accordingly that governments, non-government organizations, aid donors and researchers draw on this experience in developing 'environmental subsidiarity principles'. Some key lessons learnt to date are discussed below.

Assessing capacity

McKean (2002, p10) interpreted the subsidiarity principle as stipulating that all tasks be performed at the lowest possible level of social organization, and proposed the following technical way to know how low 'possible' is: an individual subunit of the organization system is free to undertake all the tasks that do not affect anyone in another subunit, 'but we move up a notch to a higher level if a subunit wants to engage in behavior that will affect any other subunit'. Any given task is therefore moved upwards in an organization system (i.e. centralized) until a level is reached where all individuals with an interest in the task are represented.

She illustrated this logic with a hypothetical gravity-fed irrigation system wherein irrigators draw their water from various subchannels. How the irrigators along a subchannel at the tail end of the system share the water reaching that subchannel among themselves cannot affect the water received by irrigators along any other subchannel. Hence, they are left to their own devices in performing that task. What if they were unsatisfied with the volume of water reaching their subchannel? Even if it were physically possible for them to increase that volume unilaterally (which it is not since they are at the bottom of a gravity-fed system), they would be precluded from doing so since any increase could come only from reducing the volume available to irrigators along subchannels closer to the top end of the system. The task of deciding whether the volume of water reaching the tail-end irrigators should be increased, and under what terms, would be made by a group that nests that subunit of irrigators along with the subunits (representing irrigators along 'upstream' subchannels) from which water might be reallocated. The higher-level group might decide, for instance, to allow more water to reach the tail end of the system provided the subunit that benefits pays an agreed level of compensation to the subunits from which the water is reallocated.

This interpretation of the subsidiarity principle assumes that a subunit's capacity to perform a task depends only on whether the task can be fulfilled without visiting spillovers upon other subunits. However, the capacity of a lower-level subunit to perform a task at the same standard as a higher-level subunit will typically depend also on additional factors. A subunit may be able to perform a particular task without generating spillovers, yet may be at a disadvantage compared with a higher-level subunit in accessing all the physical, financial, human and social capital needed to conduct that task to a specified standard. When this is the case, it seems reasonable to interpret the subsidiarity principle as justifying centralization of that task further than the level needed to represent all individuals with an interest in the task – but only to the minimum extent necessary to ensure that it is conducted to the required standard.

For instance, Ribot (2002) found that governments, non-governmental organizations and aid donors often have important roles to play in community-based natural resource management programmes in terms of redressing existing inequities and supporting local civic education (e.g. enabling people to understand their legal rights and responsibilities). Baland and Platteau (1996) concluded that governments can have advantages over local community-based groups in tasks like: (a) providing technical assistance or guidance; (b) establishing a legal framework which allows local groups to gain legally enforceable acknowledgement of their identity and rights; and (c) supplying formal conflict-resolution mechanisms for those occasions when groups resolving their own conflicts would be too divisive.

Baland and Platteau (ibid) discussed, for example, how customary mechanisms for conflict resolution and sanctioning had broken down in some Japanese coastal fisheries, the result being that formal mechanisms – including litigation among fishers – had assumed significant importance. They discussed also how, in 1978, the Nepalese Government introduced regulations authorizing the transfer of significant areas of public forest land to management by local communities. However, lack of widespread local knowledge of the purpose of the new strategy or of the details of managing such lands presented a major hurdle to engaging local participation in the community-based arrangements. Consequently, the Government assigned to itself tasks such as the following while this hurdle remained: establishing forest nurseries in all relevant villages; financing and training local people to run the nurseries and protect the forests; and providing extension materials to facilitate training at the grass roots level.

Catalysing capacity

Where potential exists for a subunit at any level to overcome an existing capacity shortfall, the subsidiarity principle implies an obligation on higher-level actors, including governments, to help realize that potential. Ribot (2002, p15) characterized capacity-building as a 'chicken and egg problem'. There is often reluctance to decentralize tasks to lower-level subunits before their capacity has been proven, despite the fact that it is impossible to establish such proof until decentralization has occurred.

One solution to this chicken-and-egg problem is to begin by decentralizing simpler tasks for which lower-level capacity is clearly evident and/or the costs of failure would not be severe – the strategy being to reinforce and strengthen this capacity such that further tasks, of escalating difficulty, can be decentralized over time. The experience of efforts since 1979 in the Gal Oya district of Sri Lanka to revive an abandoned irrigation system illustrates the potential of such a 'catalytic' strategy.

The Gal Oya irrigation system was the largest in the country, and reputedly also the most run down. Farmers had not found ways of cooperating to rehabilitate the scheme due to their great social and cultural heterogeneity. McKean (2002, p16) described how they were 'afflicted by a severe ethnic split, with richer Sinhalese upstream and poorer Tamils downstream, reinforcing the very damaging social stratification that causes violence in Sri Lanka to this day'. The Sri Lankan Government assigned the project of rehabilitating the system to an international agency interested in farmer self-organization (the Agrarian Research and Training Institute). This agency began collaborating with a research group at Cornell University focused on participatory development.

The combined team decided the best way forward was to help the farmers develop an organizational system they could genuinely call their own. Wijayaratna and Uphoff (1997, p166) discussed how this entailed 'making a planned intervention that was strong enough to generate an internal dynamic of the community toward local organization but controlled enough not to dominate and direct such efforts of the community'. To this end, the team recruited, trained and deployed young people they called 'institutional organizers'. The purpose of these organizers was to facilitate farmer interaction directed at solving their mutual problems, promote group identity, and thereby promote farmer self-reliance. Thus the strategy was 'demand-led', and started by getting farmers to work together informally on relatively simple problems they had jointly identified as key obstacles to further progress. It followed the motto: 'Work first, organize second' (ibid, p174). McKean (2002, p17) reported the outcome as follows:

> Each small success improved the confidence level of the farmers and led to a larger success. In this way the project and the farmers struggled, from the bottom up, to create social capital where there was none... [The] project achieved a remarkable turnaround in the functioning of the system and agricultural production, in farmer confidence in tacking all sorts of other problems, and eventually in the government's new found respect for these farmers.

Unfortunately, it has been the case too often that attempts to emulate the success of such capacity-building efforts overlook what is probably the most fundamental reason for success – the fact that the successful efforts are demand-led. Individuals can be expected to participate in capacity-building activities only to the extent that they believe this will further their goals. However, capacity-building activities are frequently supply-driven, their designs inspired too much by the preoccupations of their sponsors (e.g. in documenting outputs, like the number of training courses run) and not enough by what actually motivates target populations. Child (2003) observed that the outcome typically is a plethora of questionable training courses, sequenced inappropriately. For a target population to perceive that participation in capacity-building activities will further their goals, they must have secure rights to reap benefits from exercising the capacities developed. The farmers targeted in the Gal Oya project were motivated to participate because of their secure rights to increased water availability generated by the project – and because they already valued water highly. In many environmental projects, like those concerned with biodiversity, these favourable conditions are unlikely to exist at the outset. Often, the resources to be conserved will not already be valued highly by the people whose participation is sought. Moreover, they will typically lack rights to share in any conservation outcomes that a project achieves.

As demonstrated by Zimbabwe's CAMPFIRE (Communal Areas Management Program for Indigenous Resources) programme, however, it can be possible with institutional ingenuity to develop these favourable conditions. Until the 1970s in that country, the state took sole responsibility for conserving wildlife. Conservation benefited mainly foreign tourists and hunters, resident white Zimbabweans, and scientists. Typically, local people lost rights to access land (e.g. for forage resources) and wildlife (e.g. for hunting) when protected areas ('game reserves') were established (Metcalfe, 1997). The 1975 Parks and Wildlife Act, as amended in 1982 (two years after independence), provided legal support for the institutional innovations that CAMPFIRE would introduce. 'Appropriate authority' to manage wildlife locally was granted to district councils under the Act, provided they could convince the Department of National Parks and Wildlife Management of their 'intent and capacity' to apply such authority beneficially. Intent was ultimately demonstrated by a district council agreeing to various principles and guidelines and to a basic formula for distributing wildlife revenues. According to this formula, at least 50 per cent of such revenues would be allocated to communities for their direct benefit. With few districts experienced in managing wildlife resources, the capacity criterion remained moot. CAMPFIRE commenced in 1989 when appropriate authority status was granted to two districts: Nyaminyami and Guruve. Other districts soon realized that they too could access hunting and tourism revenues by conserving wildlife, and ten further districts successfully sought the same status by the year's end (ibid).

Child (2003) found that the growth of CAMPFIRE was due predominantly to the institutional change, through legislation, that led local people to understand that wildlife was potentially valuable to them and gave them confidence that they would be rewarded for any efforts they made to realize that potential value. Capacity-building efforts complemented the institutional change, but by themselves would not have significantly affected local behaviour. Child observed that in Namibia, for instance, on-ground progress in community-based wildlife conservation remained poor despite substantial expenditure on capacity-building activities between 1993 and 1997. It was only with enactment of new legislation in 1997, allowing communities to manage wildlife if they registered as 'conservancies', that the capacity-building investment began to show a return.

Obstacles to subsidiarity

Cases like those discussed above, where lucrative management rights are decentralized to local communities, are rare. It is more often the case that governments retain such rights for themselves, transferring only those rights with no commercial value. Meanwhile, fiscal crises are driving governments to decentralize the least lucrative and tractable problems to local levels.

Even where valuable rights are transferred, central governments often attach conditions to these transfers such that local authorities are left little discretion in how they exercise their new rights. For instance, Ribot (2002) discussed how democratically elected local governments were established in Mali and Uganda as recipients of decentralized management rights. However, the local authorities were required to use these rights in accordance with restrictive management plans imposed by environmental agencies of the central government, which in effect 're-recentralize any autonomy implied by the transfer of rights' (ibid, p7). Such restrictive control by central governments contravenes the 'principle of vindication' that Schumacher (1973) proposed to complement the subsidiarity principle. He justified the principle of vindication in the following terms: 'If a large number of criteria is laid down for accountability, every subsidiary unit can be faulted on one item or another... Unless the number of criteria for accountability is kept very small indeed, creativity and *entrepreneurship* cannot flourish' (ibid, p230, original emphasis).

Uphoff et al (1998) found from the community-based programmes of rural development they studied, for instance, that implementation of rules for allocating programme costs and benefits among individuals is more successful when communities are left with autonomy to decide these rules for themselves. To illustrate, they referred to a programme of integrated watershed management that commenced in 1991 in Rajasthan, India's north-western state. Krishna (1997) explained that the programme sought integrated solutions to problems of degraded grazing lands, reduced fodder and fuel availability in common lands and forests, and insufficient water for agriculture, fodder production and drinking. It focused on 250 watersheds, each comprising an area of 1000–2000 hectares draining to a common point. The scale of action required could not be resourced solely by government and other external sponsors. Hence, it was decided that residents of each village would contribute at least 10 per cent of the cost of on-ground actions benefiting its members, either in the form of cash or labour. Nevertheless, each village could participate in deciding rules for allocating its total cost share among its constituent households. Provision of this autonomy recognized that adaptation of inter-household cost-sharing rules to local needs and values would strengthen villagers' compliance with those rules.

The benefits of decentralizing commercially attractive management rights for mobilizing local people and developing their capacities are often also undermined by governments failing to adequately secure these changes. Decentralization decisions usually occur through ministerial decrees or administrative orders. These are less secure than decisions established in law. Ribot (2002) reported that decentralization of management powers over natural resources was called for in Mali's environmental legislation, such as the 1996 forestry code, but that this did not prevent actual decentralization decisions being left to the discretion of the ministry responsible for forests. Until so-called decentralization decisions are given the security of law, they are less concerned with effectively decentralizing rights than with delegating privileges. Thus: 'Neither local authorities nor local people will invest in the responsible exercise of powers if they believe they will not hold these powers for long... When privileges are delegated, people remain subjects of higher authorities' (ibid, p6).

Indeed, many central governments worldwide have revealed themselves as better at talking about decentralization than doing it. Their decentralization initiatives tend to be more a case of rapidly offloading responsibilities in response to fiscal crises than of seeking to empower lower levels. Andersson et al (2004) noted, for example, how Nicaragua's central government decided in 1997 to transfer some of its environmental responsibilities to municipal governments. The financial resources provided to the municipal governments to support this transfer were inadequate, however, so that few of them could exercise their new responsibilities effectively. Such attempts at 'decentralization on the cheap' have been criticized by Ostrom (2000b, p21) as follows:

> It is one thing to self-organize to create your own property and slowly develop the rules of association that enable a group to benefit from the long-term management of that resource. It is quite something else to have a government tell you that you now have to manage something that the government can no longer handle itself!

Part of this problem is that central governments, and often higher-level organizations more generally, tend to overestimate the pace at which lower-level subunits early in their life cycle can build their capacities to perform demanding tasks. Uphoff et al (1998, p33) observed that this mistake usually arises from 'a linear way of thinking about schedules, expecting to accomplish equal amounts of work during each time period, rather than having a logistic (S-shaped) curve in mind'. With this latter perspective, decentralization efforts begin gradually, allowing capacities to accumulate incrementally until a critical mass of capacity is established and the pace of decentralization can be stepped up. These authors observed how the first institutional organizers in Gal Oya were able to work with only 75–100 farmers each. Once improved techniques for communicating with farmers had been learned, and after benefits from farmers started to become evident, the organizers found that they could remain just as effective dealing with 200–300 farmers. By the project's end, when farmer organizations had been established, organizers were working on average with almost 2000 farmers each (Wijayaratna and Uphoff, 1997).

Nevertheless, the more fundamental part of the problem usually has to do with opposition to effective decentralization from vested interests. Governments and other organizations that have traditionally benefited from centralization of management rights are often reluctant to transfer or share them, at least where those rights remain useful to them in furthering their interests. Ribot (2002, p7) observed accordingly that '[o]ne of the first lessons to be learned from decentralization experiences around the world is that despite stated government commitments to decentralization, central governments and environmental ministries resist transferring appropriate and sufficient powers to local authorities'. Decentralization of valuable management rights to community organizations can limit the ability of centralized structures to pursue their own sectional interests. Indeed, the CAMPFIRE programme evolved in part from recognition that giving local people rights to share wildlife conservation revenues would lead them to fight any central government attempts to increase its share of revenues (Child, 2003).

Not surprisingly, therefore, central governments tend to be wary of catalysing 'people power' through effective decentralization. Baland and Platteau (1996, p379) commented on how governments in many developing countries seek to control attempts by local communities to organize themselves, 'particularly so if these attempts result in the development of large scale grassroots movements or networks or in assertion of claims for more autonomy'. Control of this kind might involve trying to influence the selection of leaders for local organizations, or to co-opt or buy off the leaders who are selected locally. It can also involve playing 'divide and rule' with the grass roots itself (Uphoff et al, 1998).

Strategic behaviour by governments in responding to pressures for decentralized environmental decision making is not limited to developing countries, as Lane's (2003) account of the Regional Forest Agreements (RFA) process in Australia makes clear. The objective of the process was to resolve seemingly intractable conflicts around the nation over public native forests through collaborative methods of resource assessment. This would be achieved by the RFAs simultaneously providing resource security for extractive industries, conserving ecologically important areas, and protecting indigenous and other values in the management of these forests. Government rhetoric emphasized the importance of inclusively decentralizing rights to participate in the development of RFAs, but actual decentralization fell well short of this ideal. Probably the most important reason for this, according to Lane, was the emphasis governments placed on scientific rigour in the assessment and decision making process. This emphasis allowed participation opportunities to become dominated by constituencies with pre-existing capacities to engage in conventional scientific discourse, typically logging and anti-logging interests. Other, including indigenous, interests were thereby largely excluded from the process. Moreover, opportunities for inclusive participation were not provided at key stages of the process. The outcomes were summarized as follows:

> [T]he extent of decentralization of real authority by the state to civic actors was highly selective and capricious... While state agencies in this case found it useful to promote a formal policy rhetoric that suggested the process would centrally involve civic engagement and dispute resolution, decentralizing authority to genuinely broadly based deliberative processes might have been too conceptually and politically challenging for institutions used to centralized policy control... The state sought finality to a public policy conflict that had been acrimonious, long running, and electorally difficult... Public deliberation was suborned by private interests and a wide range of other actors with legitimate claims to and interests in the public forest resource were marginalized (ibid, p291).

Consider also the account by Sproule-Jones (2002) of experiences with institutional reform to repair the degraded environments of 43 Areas of Concern (bays, harbours and river mouths) along the shorelines of the Great Lakes in North America. In 1985, the Governments of Canada and the US were requested by the International Joint Commission (established in 1909 by those governments to address their transborder problems) to develop remedial action plans (RAPs) for each of the 43 areas. The federal governments were required to involve local stakeholders in the plan development process, although they were given autonomy in choosing stakeholders and in designing the rules under which their interests would be accounted for. Public officials running the RAP programme made much of the programme's achievements in the direction of engaging stakeholder participation. For instance, one group of officials wrote of the RAP programme that:

> different organizations, agencies and stakeholders [are viewed as] equal members of a team... Sharing decision-making power and accepting responsibility for action is requisite, as no single agency or organization has the capacity to plan and implement RAPs (Hartig et al, 1995, p8 as quoted in Sproule-Jones, 2002, p106).

The reality of power sharing was decidedly less generous. The state and provincial governments that were empowered, in collaboration with their federal counterparts, to design institutional arrangements for the programme were content with establishing stakeholder organizations to provide them with input to decisions made elsewhere. The RAPs developed were layered into pre-existing government programmes. Hence, 'it was the interests of the lead agency (or agencies) that prevailed... RAPs had the potential to change powers and immunities. However, they were designed to maintain existing powers and immunities' (Sproule-Jones, 2002, p109).

Reluctance of central governments, and higher-level organizations more generally, to support effective decentralization often also arises from the influence of Progressive beliefs on how they perceive the capacities of lower levels to perform certain tasks satisfactorily. Berger and Neuhaus (1996, p148) referred to this general problem as one of 'sluggish mindsets', with people accustomed to thinking along Progressive lines 'not easily induced to look at reality in new ways'. Ribot (2002, p7) observed accordingly that the resistance of central governments to effectively decentralizing natural resource management 'can reflect genuine, but often misguided or vague, concerns about maintaining standards, social and environmental well-being, and political stability'.

Progressive beliefs remain influential in the public policy discourse surrounding subsidiarity, decentralization and environmental management. As explained in Chapter 1, this is due in significant measure to the success of mainstream microeconomics in establishing intellectual legitimacy and public acceptance for a market-based model of public policy formulation founded on those beliefs. The logic of mainstream microeconomics leads us to conclude that actors sharing large-group problems of collective action cannot solve them for themselves, and must consequently allow higher-level actors to solve such problems for them. Interpretation of the subsidiarity principle through the lens of such logic thereby subverts its original devolutionary spirit. Frey and Eichenberger (1999, p60) remarked accordingly that its inclusion in the Amsterdam Treaty has not been:

> a strong constraint to centralization. There is hardly a government activity for which it cannot be argued that it causes some transnational spillovers... Therefore the [European Commission] can always argue that centralization is compatible with the subsidiarity principle.

Overcoming the obstacles

Although vested interests and sluggish mindsets frequently present formidable obstacles to effective decentralization, they are normally not insurmountable. Uphoff et al (1998, p177) found that enduring success in coping with such obstacles depends on 'maintaining a strategic long-term view and commitment, grounded on solid support from rural populations, and balanced by short-term tactical moves that build up goodwill and blunt attacks'. Demonstrating good performance can be a particularly powerful way of turning opposition into support, even if only of a grudging kind. Alternatively, opposition might be avoided by 'flying below the radar' until enough capacity evolves to withstand or outmanoeuvre it. Thus: 'Many successful rural programs have commenced work quietly and unobtrusively, with a minimum of publicity. The organization's profile has been raised only at a later stage' (ibid, p187). Another way, often used to win over higher-level support for effective decentralization, involves the formation of alliances. Such alliances can allow the bottom to co-opt the top. Hence: 'Strong support... is not necessary from the outset. This can be built over time... With good performance, others who initially opposed the venture have reason to come around' (ibid, p190).

The history of Zimbabwe's CAMPFIRE programme, as recounted by Child (2003), shows that the strategy of building alliances in support of effective decentralization requires not only patience but also anticipation of eventual counter-moves by those the strategy seeks to outflank. Networking among southern Africa's leading conservationists during the early 1970s established momentum for the idea that wildlife had potential to become a profitable and major private land use. The emergence of wildlife as a commercial use of private land offered confidence that it could also be competitive on the more marginal lands found in Rhodesia's (now Zimbabwe's) communal areas. In the mid-1970s, that country's Department of National Parks and Wildlife Management (DNPWLM) persuaded its Minister to dedicate revenues from three game reserves to the local populations. The Department recognized that the government of that time was not ready to accept local people earning wildlife revenues directly, and that getting revenues returned to them bureaucratically was a useful step in the right direction.

By 1989, that earlier strategic move had helped to bring about a policy climate conducive to launching the CAMPFIRE programme and, thereby, granting 12 District Councils authority to control wildlife within each of their jurisdictions and obtain direct access to a share of associated wildlife revenues. The programme was led originally by the CAMPFIRE Collaborative Group, chaired initially by the DNPWLM (the other members including the Zimbabwe Trust – a non-governmental organization focused on rural development – and sections of the University of Zimbabwe and the World Wide Fund for Nature). This Group supported a series of workshops out of which the CAMPFIRE Association (of wildlife-producing districts) was established. At a further workshop in 1992, the Group agreed that the Association should become lead agency for the programme (Metcalfe, 1997).

This significant progress towards effective decentralization – as a consequence of enlightened government professionals with policy making influence allying themselves with civil organizations better equipped for community capacity building – was facilitated by the open-mindedness and excitement of the immediate post-independence era. However, this window of opportunity was closing by the early 1990s, with centralizing forces in the bureaucracy having regrouped. Moreover, the alliance of professionals responsible for these developments was largely white, and became out-manoeuvred by reactive bureaucrats partly as a consequence of failing to adequately provide for succession of their roles to like-minded black professionals. According to Child (2003), this experience also highlights the importance, once an opportunity for effective decentralization presents itself, of responding to local community needs for capacity building quickly enough that the communities' decentralized rights can use success to argue against eventual pressures for recentralization.

Core challenge 2: Ensuring complementarity in how tasks are conducted

Motivation

The previous section was concerned with the first of two core challenges in solving multi-scale environmental problems through nested organizational systems; namely, the challenge of allocating tasks optimally across different organizational levels. In this section, we proceed to the second of these challenges: ensuring that the tasks allocated across such organizational systems are conducted in ways that complement one another.

Complementarity of actions by different actors spread across a nested organizational system can arise from both cooperation and competition between them, but only to the extent that incentives exist for this to occur (Ostrom et al, 1999b). This is the gist of Schumacher's (1973, p232) 'principle of motivation' for the large-scale organization, which is based on the 'truism that people act in accordance with their motives'. As obvious as this principle seems, he remarked on how frequently the design of multi-level organizational systems proceeds without sufficient appreciation of its implications.

When attention is paid to the principle of motivation in the design of nested organizational systems, the primary focus is usually on incentives generated through financial instruments. Such an instrument was applied successfully by the National Irrigation Administration (NIA) Program in the Philippines when it needed, after termination of a World Bank-assisted project, to support with user fees the scaling-up of its efforts to institutionalize participatory farmer management of irrigation systems. Earlier attempts by the NIA to get community-based organizations ('irrigation associations') to collect service fees from farmers to cover the operating and maintenance costs of irrigation systems were frustrated by farmer resistance borne of expectations, based on previous experiences, that politicians would eventually come through with the funds needed to keep the systems running.

This situation was turned around significantly in the late 1980s when the NIA introduced contractual arrangements giving irrigation associations strong financial incentives to collect as high a proportion as possible of the service fees due from their constituent farmers. Under these arrangements, an irrigation association retained a share of the total amount of fees it collected provided total collections exceeded 50 per cent of the total amount due. Two per cent could be retained from collections up to 60 per cent of the total due; five per cent from collections between 60 and 70 per cent; ten per cent from collections between 70 and 90 per cent; and 15 per cent from collections above 90 per cent. Not only were irrigation associations motivated to pursue fee collection more vigorously as a result. Farmers were also more motivated to pay the fees under these arrangements, once they saw the fees translating into better operation of their local irrigation systems and thus into higher irrigation-derived incomes for themselves (Bagadion, 1997; Uphoff et al, 1998).

Accountability

Too often, however, the efficacy of incentive instruments intended to motivate local actors to perform the tasks decentralized to them is low as a result of failures to enforce the conditions giving the instruments their motivational potential. Without such accountability, local actors will often pursue their own interests at the expense of the wider collective interest. For an example, consider Andersson's (2003) account of decentralization reforms in Bolivia's forestry sector. The 1996 Forestry Law in that country gave municipal governments direct control over 25 per cent of royalties centrally collected within their respective territories from commercial logging concessions, in return for which they were required to perform a range of tasks. The main task involved monitoring and enforcing the formal rules stipulated by the Forestry Law. A further key task entailed demarcation of public forested lands in the municipal territory to be used exclusively for local communities. Another involved providing technical assistance to local forest users in order that they might develop forest management plans and acquire formal forest property rights. The reality, however, was that municipal governments continued to receive their share of royalties regardless of whether they performed the tasks required of them. A survey reported by Andersson (ibid) found that 78 per cent of the mayors of the municipal governments perceived that monitoring visits by the central government occurred rarely or never. Regression analysis of the survey data suggested that the strength of the mayors' perceptions that central government monitoring was occurring had a marked positive effect on the likelihood of their municipal governments undertaking the forestry sector tasks expected of them. This finding was consistent with the findings of other studies reported in Andersson (ibid) to the effect that only about half the municipal governments receiving forestry royalties had performed some required tasks, and less than 10 per cent had satisfied all requirements.

Adequately monitored and enforced, formal instruments have an important role to play in creating the incentives needed to induce complementary actions across a nested organizational system. However, it is typically the case that the transaction costs of providing adequate levels of monitoring and enforcement of such instruments become unaffordable unless much of the target population is already prepared to act as needed. Often, therefore, the actual contribution of formal incentive instruments to creating needed incentives depends on whether they are supported by other measures that reduce to an affordable level the need for the instruments to be monitored and enforced by third parties.

With the NIA programme in the Philippines, for example, the efficacy of the 'sliding scale' financial incentives in motivating irrigation associations to collect service fees from farmers followed in part from the programme's success in engaging farmer participation in managing the irrigation systems and, thereby, developing their sense of responsibility to help implement management decisions. In respect of financial management, the willingness of farmers to cooperate with efforts by their irrigation associations to collect service fees from them was strengthened by the participatory arrangements in place to help farmers keep their associations financially accountable. Central to these arrangements were the general meetings of farmers that each irrigation association held at the beginning and end of each cropping season. These meetings gave special emphasis to preparing the association's annual budget and presenting accounts explaining its financial situation. These measures served to gain farmers' trust that their irrigation association would utilize its revenues, including from service fees, in ways that benefited them. Without this trust, the costs of collecting service fees from many farmers may well have overwhelmed the encouragement that the incentive arrangements gave the associations to step up their collection efforts.

Andersson's (ibid) study of the decentralization reforms in Bolivia's forestry sector provides further evidence of how accountability pressures from the grass roots can help realize the intended motivational effects of financial incentives introduced from the centre, at least when the incentives are aligned with grass roots preferences. Regression analysis of his survey data suggested that greater efforts by constituents of municipal governments to hold them accountable in discharging their forestry management responsibilities had a significant positive affect on the probability of the responsibilities being carried out.

A further strategy for reducing the need for formal provision of accountability mechanisms to realize the motivational potential of incentive instruments involves harnessing competition as a means of bringing about monitoring and enforcement by the parties seeking to benefit from the instruments. This strategy is illustrated by the operations of the Six-S Association, as described by Lecomte and Krishna (1997) and Uphoff et al (1998). This is a non-governmental organization promoting rural development in the Sahel region of West Africa – particularly by supporting voluntary village groups to undertake development work during the region's long dry season when the predominantly agricultural population has little other work to do. The development work supported has included natural resource management projects like building dams and wells to conserve water, constructing contour stone barriers to conserve soil and water within fields, and planting village woodlots. The Six-S Association was established in 1977, and by the late 1980s was serving hundreds of thousands of people. These people were organized into 3000 groups, located in 1500 villages. The groups were federated into zones (each encompassing 10–50 groups), with the zones federated into 75 regions.

Planning of the projects to be supported by Six-S began with the village level groups. Each group would submit its plan to an assembly of groups in its zone. The assembly would consider all plans. It would then allocate among all proposed projects the funds distributed to the zone by the Six-S Association from donor grants. Part of the funds allocated to each project was in the form of a loan. Allocation decisions were based on criteria agreed by the assembly. The groups became motivated to monitor each other's repayment of loans because funds repaid became available for recycling to other groups. This 'is a powerful factor in knitting together the village groups in a network of mutual responsibility and assistance' (Lecomte and Krishna, 1997, p87). Hence,

Uphoff et al (1998, p92) remarked in relation to this case that '[t]he central office has no need to police the use of funds when member groups are competing in terms of ... activities that they are in the best position to assess'.

The benefits of competition for realizing the potential of a financial instrument to motivate complementary actions across a nested organizational system are illustrated also by Ostrom's (1990) account of the operations of the Central and West Basin Water Replenishment District ('District') in the US state of California. In 1959, this enterprise was created by groundwater producers operating, and approved by citizens residing, in that region. This enterprise was empowered under California's Water Replenishment District Act to undertake activities contributing to replenishment of depleted reserves of groundwater within its jurisdiction, and to primarily finance these activities by taxing each groundwater producer according to its assessed extractions. Aside from purchasing water from outside that jurisdiction to use for the purpose of groundwater replenishment, the District was responsible for operation of the works involved in utilizing the purchased water for that purpose. It was required under its Act to investigate the competitiveness of contracting other enterprises to operate those works before deciding to undertake that task itself. The outcome was that the Los Angeles County Flood Control District ('County') was commissioned to operate the replenishment works. This decision was made in the knowledge that scope for the County to exercise monopoly powers in this relationship, and thereby subvert the effectiveness of the contractual arrangement in motivating it to act in the District's best interests, was limited by the District having access to several other potentially competitive operators of the replenishment works and also the option of appointing its own staff to operate the works.

Leadership

Leadership is another key to increasing the effectiveness of a formal instrument in delivering the incentives it is designed to establish. Leadership can bring about the convergence of individual actors' values towards the shared values reflected in such an instrument, thereby increasing the proportion of actors seeing voluntary compliance with the instrument's conditions to be in their own best interests. Selin and Chavez (1995, p191) defined a leader as some party 'whose energy and vision mobilizes others to participate'. Uphoff et al (1998, p73) concluded that leadership was one of the most important variables responsible for success in the 30 decentralized programmes of rural development (including natural resource management) they studied: 'The kinds of persons who come to fill the responsible roles in [local rural development] organizations have as much influence on performance as the structuring of these roles – their authority, their control over financial resources, and so forth'. They found that successful large-scale programmes were often characterized by a collective concept of leadership, rather than one fixated on individuals. For instance, the NIA in the Philippines sought strong and committed leadership at all levels of its programme, with at least one leader for each ten members (Bagadion, 1997).

As Uphoff et al (1998) found from their study of rural development experiences, much of the power of leaders to influence others' values derives from their willingness and ability to exemplify the kinds of values they would like to see adopted. They observed, for instance, 'how important it is, if egalitarian and participatory farmer organizations are to be fostered, that the agency promoting them exhibit such values and modes of operation' (ibid, p95). Krishna's (1997) account of Rajasthan's programme of participatory watershed management demonstrates that it is quite possible for government agencies to align their internal cultures with the values they expect actors in participatory initiatives to embrace. The government agency in that case – Rajasthan's department of watershed development and soil conservation – had been established only four months prior to commencement of field work for the watershed programme. Within a few months, the department had convened four three-day workshops attended by the leaders of the department's 97 field units. At these conferences, the objectives and programming needs of the new watershed management programme were discussed 'in an open, semistructured manner, with everyone contributing, regardless of seniority' (ibid, p259). The department also held extensive debriefing sessions at the end of the programme's first planting season. Staff reported progress in developing area-specific technologies and in identifying local practices with potential for wider application. They exchanged what they had learned about initiating participatory processes of dialogue among villagers. In addition, the effectiveness of the programme's first year of implementation was discussed in participatory meetings where staff throughout the department contributed towards development of its ongoing implementation strategy.

One critical implementation obstacle faced early on by the department arose from inadequate preparation of its field-level staff to exercise decentralized decision making responsibilities. With such decentralization signifying 'a major inversion in a bureaucracy steeped in top-down tradition' (ibid, p263), many of the staff expected to accept increased responsibilities initially lacked the confidence and motivation needed to do so effectively. The department responded to this challenge by making each staff member in the field responsible for all the planning and implementation tasks in a single microwatershed. The needs of such staff for cross-disciplinary knowledge were satisfied through provision of training. The confidence, morale and motivation of field staff were strengthened by combining them into units of seven to ten individuals. Unit members were jointly responsible for a group of watersheds, and relied upon one another for technical advice and moral support. Added motivation to support one another arose from the department measuring performance primarily at the unit level. Unit members were also motivated by the fact that units had been given substantial authority over planning and implementation within their respective groups of watersheds. Hence, they could devote their energies to these activities with considerable confidence that their decisions would not be overturned higher up in their department. As Uphoff et al (1998) found more generally, '[t]he satisfactions from contributing to a successful operation ... can themselves be substantial and motivating'.

Key lessons from the cases reviewed

A range of lessons for designing nested organizational systems to address complex environmental problems were brought together in this chapter. The main lessons identified are listed below. Two categories of lessons are distinguished, corresponding to the two challenges that Young (2002b) located at the heart of the problem of designing nested organizational systems.

Lessons for allocating tasks across organizational levels

The main lessons in this category were:

- Allocate tasks across organizational levels in accordance with the principle of subsidiarity; that is, decentralize each task to the lowest level with the capacity to conduct it satisfactorily
- The capacity at a given organizational level to conduct a task satisfactorily depends partly on whether all actors with an interest in the task are represented at that level. Subsidiarity requires, therefore, that a task not be decentralized to the point that some actors with an interest in the task cease to be represented
- The capacity at a given level to perform a task satisfactorily depends also on whether there is sufficient access at that level to all the physical, financial, human and social capital needed to achieve that standard of performance
- The capacity at a given level to perform a task satisfactorily can often be increased through strategies seeking to strengthen access to the requisite capital by catalysing the relevant increasing-return dynamics. Subsidiarity obliges actors at higher levels to explore such opportunities before ruling out the possibility of decentralizing tasks to lower levels. At the same time, it cautions against over-optimistic expectations of how quickly lower-level capacities to cope with decentralization can be developed
- Actors tend to participate in activities designed to build their capacities only when they expect participation to help further their goals. Hence, capacity-building efforts are unlikely to succeed unless the target population has secure rights to benefit from the capacities developed
- Subunits assigned tasks in accordance with the subsidiarity principle should be allowed as much autonomy as possible in how they decide to conduct those tasks
- Higher-level actors tend to resist effective decentralization, partly because of perceived self-interest but also due to sincere scepticism arising from deeply-ingrained Progressive beliefs. When effective decentralization does occur, this is often due to strategic efforts to overcome this resistance. Success in such efforts tends to rely considerably on the ability of lower-level actors to mobilize a bandwagon of support from actors at higher levels. This ability often depends on building up an impressive track record.

Lessons for ensuring cross-level complementarity in the conduct of tasks

In this category, the main lessons were:

- Tasks allocated among different actors will be conducted in complementary ways only to the extent that incentives exist for this to occur. A range of incentive types exist. For instance, incentives may be monetary (e.g. project funding), social (e.g. peer approval) or psychological (e.g. self-satisfaction). While this lesson may seem trite, designers of large-scale organizational systems often give it insufficient thought
- Financial instruments are an important way of establishing such incentives, but succeed in doing so only to the extent that recipients of incentive payments comply with the conditions attached to those payments
- While monitoring and enforcement systems are typically needed to bolster compliance with conditions attached to incentive payments, they are often insufficient by themselves to achieve anything like full compliance. The reach of such systems is limited in many cases by the transaction costs of operating them
- Opportunities for actors at any level to participate in the design and administration of incentive instruments affecting them can increase their voluntary compliance with instrument conditions, and thereby support efforts to ensure compliance through monitoring and enforcement systems
- The load on monitoring and enforcement systems in this area can also be reduced by designing incentive instruments such that ongoing competition within the target population for incentive payments increases informal pressures on its members to comply with payment conditions
- Leadership is another important means of strengthening voluntary compliance with incentive instruments. Leaders can have a particularly powerful influence in this regard when they act as role models for the kinds of values and behaviours they seek to inspire. Leadership is not necessarily limited to isolated individuals. It may be exercised, for instance, by a network of like-minded individuals spread across an organizational system, or by an alliance of forward-thinking individuals at one level of the system (e.g. within one section of a government agency).

This set of key lessons from international cases for designing collaborative systems of environmental management as nested systems is no doubt incomplete, and it is hoped others will be spurred to fill the gaps. Moreover, these lessons must be regarded as tentative until such time as they can be corroborated by a wider range of experiences. As Moore and Koontz (2003, p452) remarked recently, hesitancy in generalizing from particular cases of collaborative environmental management to theory is well justified 'given the newness of the phenomenon and the relatively early stage of research on it'. However, this does not mean that attempts at this stage to learn from experiences in collaborative environment management are premature. It means only that any lesson gained should be given the status of hypothesis rather than theory. This status is far from insignificant. Without hypotheses, the systematic process of policy experimentation envisaged by proponents of adaptive management would not be possible.

From Antagonism to Trust: Collaborative Salinity Management in Australia's Murray Darling Basin

One response to the challenge of drawing lessons from experience for use in moving adaptively towards successful systems of collaborative environmental management was reported in the previous chapter. The focus there was on learning from patterns observed across cases previously documented. A complementary response is reported in this chapter. The focus here shifts to a case study by the author of a single programme of collaborative environmental management. The study explored how the developments in collective action theory discussed particularly in Chapter 3 can facilitate understanding of, and learning from, the behaviour of actors in such a programme. The study was primarily concerned with investigating the relevance in the case setting of the social capital, and particularly trust, that these developments highlight as pivotal for meaningful collaboration. The study was concerned also with identifying the particular kinds of trust that were relevant, as well as key structural variables influencing these kinds of trust. Knowledge of this kind is crucial for these developments in collective action theory to be of practical value to policy makers and practitioners.

The case in question involves a community-based collaborative programme initiated to address salinization and waterlogging problems associated with irrigation in one region of the Murray Darling Basin in south-east Australia. This Basin represents the nation's largest and most developed river system. It encompasses over one million square kilometres of land from the River Murray mouth in South Australia to southern Queensland. Around three-quarters of the nation's irrigation occurs within its boundaries. Over substantial areas of the Basin's irrigated lands, watertables have risen to within 2 metres of the soil surface, as a result of both native vegetation clearance and application of irrigation water, resulting in salinization as well as waterlogging. It was estimated in 1987 that 96,000 hectares were affected by saline soils and 560,000 hectares were underlain by watertables within 2 metres of the surface. By 2040, the area of irrigated land affected by salinization and waterlogging due to high watertables is expected to reach 1.3 million hectares (Murray Darling Basin Commission, undated). The Murray Darling Basin is not alone in experiencing such problems, and in attempting to address them through community-based collaborative programmes. The United Nations Environment Programme (2002) reported 1995 Food and Agriculture Organization (FAO) estimates that 25–30 million hectares of the world's 255 million hectares of irrigated land were severely degraded by soil salinization.

This chapter continues, in the next section, with background information on the collaborative programme explored in the case study – a programme responsible for developing and implementing what became known as the Murray Land and Water Management Plans (LWMPs). The method of the case study is then described. We then proceed to the study findings, beginning with a discussion of the low levels of trust, and high levels of political conflict, between the NSW Government and farmers in the case setting prior to commencement of the LWMP programme. We turn then to the role of governmental and farming community leadership in bringing about sufficient escape from this 'locked in' mutual mistrust so that the first steps towards authentic collaboration in the LWMP programme could take place. The challenge of broadening community trust in, and cooperation with, the programme is then explored. The focus in the next two sections shifts to consideration of some key issues influencing government–community collaboration during the plan-development and plan-implementation phases of the programme, respectively. In the penultimate section we explore how decentralization of responsibilities for ensuring implementation of the LWMPs to a common property regime affected the propensity of farmers – as co-owners of that regime – to cooperate with efforts to monitor and enforce their compliance with the LWMPs. The chapter ends with a discussion of the kinds of trust that were found to be relevant for successful community–government collaboration in the case setting and of the key structural variables found to influence these kinds of trust.

Study background and method

The Murray Land and Water Management Plans

The case study focused on a programme of developing and implementing LWMPs for four adjoining irrigation districts in south-west New South Wales (NSW, a state in eastern Australia). Considerable decentralization of rights and responsibilities for natural resources management occurred in this programme. Indeed, the programme resulted in a company co-owned by the irrigators in these districts – Murray Irrigation Limited (MIL), in effect a common property regime – being decentralized considerable autonomy to decide how the LWMPs would be implemented.

This company is incorporated under the (NSW) Irrigation Corporations Act, 1994. It co-signed a Heads of Agreement (HoA) with the NSW Government ('Government') in 1996, and as a result was decentralized various property rights required to ensure that landholders in its area of operation comply with an agreement regarding allocation of the costs of implementing the LWMPs. The adjoining districts covered by these plans are known as Berriquin, Denimein, Wakool and Cadell, respectively. They are situated within the broad 'riverine' floodplain of the River Murray. Deniliquin, a town located near the centre of the combined area, lies about 750 kilometres south-west from Sydney, the capital of NSW. The farm area within the irrigation schemes associated with these districts is 749,202 hectares. The number of farm businesses within the schemes has been estimated at 1610 (Murray Irrigation Limited, 1998). Across the four LWMP Districts, around half of the farm area has been developed for irrigation. Most irrigation water is applied to rice crops, followed by annual pastures and perennial pastures.

During the 1980s, concerns regarding productivity losses from soil salinization and waterlogging within the districts – associated with rising watertables – attracted increasing attention from the Government and the Murray Darling Basin Ministerial Council (MDBMC). This Council was established in 1985 to integrate governmental decision making affecting the water resources of the Basin, and comprises Ministers representing the water, land and environmental portfolios of governments for the states of NSW, Victoria, South Australia and Queensland (i.e. states with land in the Basin) and of the nation's federal (or 'Commonwealth') government. Also attracting greater attention were the negative water quality consequences of discharging increasingly saline drainage from the irrigation schemes into watercourses flowing eventually into the River Murray. In response to these broader concerns, the MDBMC introduced in 1990 a Salinity and Drainage Policy that established limits on the rights of all states in the Basin to drain saline waters into the River Murray system. Around the same time, the Council also introduced a Natural Resources Management Strategy. This signalled that the Council's executive arm, the Murray Darling Basin Commission (MDBC), would no longer fund state governments to undertake salinity management programmes in the Basin unless genuine collaboration in the programmes between state governments and affected communities could be demonstrated.

As a result of these policy initiatives, landholders in the irrigation schemes, and also the Government, reconsidered how they had been trying to deal with their problems of soil salinization and waterlogging. By June 1992, the communities of each of the four districts had convened public meetings, and it was agreed in each case that a LWMP would be developed on the basis of inclusive stakeholder collaboration led by a community working group (CWG).

Negotiations between the Government and the communities of the four districts over the final shape of the LWMPs, including cost sharing arrangements, occurred during September 1995. The Government made a commitment around that time to contribute $A116 million over the first 15 years of implementing the four LWMPs, provided that the Commonwealth Government met half this cost and landholders in each district delivered on their cost sharing commitments for each year. Over 30 years, these landholder commitments sum to $A382 million. The vast majority of this commitment is 'in kind', in the form of costs incurred by landholders in fulfilling the targets for adoption of the on-farm land and water conservation practices specified in their respective district's LWMP. A diversity of on-farm practices were included in the LWMPs, including establishment of perennial pastures, upgrading farmers' groundwater pumps, installation of drainage reuse systems, and so on. In addition, the cost sharing arrangements involved levying landholders between $A0.50 and 3.15 per megalitre of their irrigation entitlements to help finance district-level works and measures (e.g. extension of district-level surface drainage networks). The on-farm adoption targets set in the LWMPs were nearly always specified for farm businesses at the district level (e.g. a total number of drainage recirculation systems to be installed across a district) rather than for individual farms. Hence, a collective action problem remained in so far as individual landholders were left scope to free ride on one another's in-kind contributions to solving their shared salinity and waterlogging problems.

In March 1995, the irrigation schemes were privatized by the Government as part of a national process of water policy reform. This left the schemes the property of MIL, which became the largest privately-owned irrigation supply and drainage company in Australia. Shares in this company were apportioned among irrigators in proportion to their irrigation entitlements. The company's assets (e.g. licence to divert irrigation water from the River Murray system, and irrigation supply and drainage infrastructure) therefore represent common property shared among its irrigator co-owners. A key condition of the HoA signed in 1996 is that the company must ensure implementation of the four LWMPs in order to retain the operating licence it requires to stay in business. It was anticipated that the company would enforce compliance by individual irrigators with the LWMPs by attaching conditions to its water-supply agreements with each of them (Schroo, 1998).

The Board of MIL established an Environment Committee to advise it on matters relating to implementation of the LWMPs. The four CWGs (renamed Community Implementation Groups for the implementation phase) provide feedback and advice regarding LWMP implementation to the Board via this Committee. They assumed the important role of suggesting, on the basis of consultation with their constituents, ways to improve their LWMPs when new knowledge came to light or old assumptions were found to be unrealistic. Minor changes could be approved by the Deniliquin-based Murray LWMP Committee comprising MIL, the Department of Land and Water Conservation (DLWC), and representatives of a company appointed to independently audit the programme. Substantial changes could be approved only by the Land and Water Management Planning Assessment Team (LWMPAT), a Sydney-based committee consisting of representatives from relevant Government agencies.

Study method

The case study method treats cases as experiments from which insights can be generalized to theoretical propositions (Yin, 1984). One approach commonly followed in applying this method is methodological triangulation, where both qualitative and quantitative data collection methods are utilized in a complementary fashion (Easterby-Smith et al, 1991). Qualitative methods seek to gather data that 'capture[s] the richness of detail and nuance of the phenomena being studied' (Hussey and Hussey, 1997, p56). Hence, they tend to use data obtained in a manner less standardized than is the case with quantitative methods. In this way, they allow issues and perspectives to be explored that might not originally have been anticipated. Quantitative methods, in contrast, seek to concentrate on measuring numerically the phenomena of interest. They emphasize the collection of data in a standardized way in order to facilitate replication.

This strategy of methodological triangulation was followed in the present case study. The qualitative research involved in-depth semi-structured interviews during 1999 with 30 key informants. The aim in selecting key informants was to choose an illustrative sample. Hence, they came from categories of people that theory, together with prior knowledge of context, indicated were relevant. The key informants selected included landholders, community leaders, the coordinator of the LWMP programme, staff from the MDBC, staff from relevant agencies of the Government (located in the region as well as in head office), MIL directors and staff, chairpersons and executive officers (past and present) of the Murray Catchment Management Committee (a community-based group responsible for advising the Government on natural resource management issues over the region that includes the area covered by the LWMP programme), a local government councillor, and a consultant with substantial involvement in the programme.

The quantitative research involved estimation of multiple regression models using data from a survey of 235 randomly-selected farm businesses located within the study area. The purpose of this research was to statistically test various hypotheses suggested by collective action theory regarding the determinants of individual farmer cooperation in implementing the LWMPs, both in terms of adopting the on-farm practices included in the LWMPs and supporting MIL in ensuring that other farmers adopt these practices. The quantitative research has been reported previously in Marshall (2004a; 2004b). The focus in this chapter is accordingly on the qualitative analysis, the findings of which are discussed below.

Study findings

Locked-in mistrust between Government and the farming community

Prior to the LWMP programme, the relationship between the irrigator community in the study area and the Government in respect of how the irrigation schemes were run had long been soured by deep-seated antagonism and mistrust. The irrigators resented the Government operating the schemes paternalistically. Daniel Liphuyzen, the chairperson, of the Denimein Community Implementation Group (CIG) at the time of interviewing and previously a member of the CWG, referred to 'the entrenched bureaucratic attitude of reluctance to change' and characterized the typical response of water bailiffs (i.e. the government staff responsible for the day-to-day operation of the schemes) to suggested improvements in the running of the schemes as 'I hope this doesn't mean more work for us. How are we supposed to do it? It's just not on'. Kelvin Baxter – an irrigator, a Director of MIL at the time of interviewing, and its first Chairperson – discussed how:

New technology just hadn't been taken up at all. The Government was still running the scheme as in 1938 when it was first built. We saw the need for change in the way the scheme was operated. It was a very labour-intensive scheme. That suited Government at the time. It was a shocking example of a government trading enterprise really... I mean it was very much an employment agency.

Consistent with these views from irrigators, Warren Martin – Deputy Director of the NSW Department of Water Resources (DWR, the predecessor of DLWC as the government agency chiefly associated with the irrigation schemes and the LWMP programme) during the time the LWMPs were developed – observed that:

I think that the irrigation areas and districts were seen a bit within the Department as being Government-owned operations. There was a bit of an attitude that we know best. That was there, there's no question about that.

Peter Stewart, who was Program Coordinator for the plan-development phase of the LWMP programme, commented similarly that:

the old Department of Water Resources people used to rule with an iron fist. They had been like that for many years. There was a culture of 'them and us'. 'Them' was the Government and it laid the law down. And 'us' were the people who paid the water bills and did what they were told.

The irrigators in the region had responded to this Progressive paternalism by Government through forming the Southern Riverina Irrigation Districts' Council (SRIDC) to press their concerns in the political domain. Mr Martin remarked how in the 1980s:

There was a fair degree of antagonism between the SRIDC and the Water Resources Commission [predecessor to the DWR] at that stage. You'd go to meetings and there was shouting across the floor... The SRIDC viewed the Commission, and the executive of the Commission at that stage... as a very antagonistic group. The SRIDC played the politics pretty hard.

Escaping lock-in with leadership

As noted above, the Government's decision in the early 1990s to address the study region's watertable related problems in collaboration with the region's community was influenced strongly by the MDBMC's Natural Resources Management Strategy. Forging genuine collaboration would not be easy given the mistrust that had 'locked in' between the DWR and the region's irrigators.

As Mr Martin observed:

> [T]he Department [of Water Resources] was not necessarily supportive of full community participation at that time. It wasn't only the irrigators that you had to bring around, to get greater community participation. A number of irrigator leaders wanted to participate, but there was still some resistance within the Department. There was still a hands-on tell-them-what-they-should-do mentality to a degree.

It seems from a number of irrigators interviewed that committed leadership by Mr Martin and some other government officers played a major part in lessening this bureaucratic resistance. This helped irrigator leaders to gain trust that collaborating with Government in addressing the salinity and waterlogging problems would be worthwhile. For instance, Gordon Ball – who had been Chairperson of the Berriquin CWG and was a Director of Murray Irrigation when interviewed – commented that Mr Martin's early involvement gave leaders of the Berriquin irrigation community confidence that the collaborative process envisaged for the LWMP programme could work. Likewise, Noel Graham and Gerard Lahy – Chairpersons of the Cadell and Wakool CIGs, respectively, when interviewed – remarked independently on the crucial importance of Mr Martin acting as their 'champion' within the higher levels of Government. Not only was he approachable, but they had confidence in his 'vision' for the partnership and that he would stick by his word once he gave it. Indeed, they were satisfied in retrospect that Government actions usually had been delivered as he said they would.

For his part, Mr Martin explained that working to make himself known personally to the leaders of the irrigator communities and taking an active interest in their ideas and concerns played a large part in winning some degree of trust from them. He observed that gaining trust:

> takes a long time. You've got to build it up. They've got to be confident that you know what you're talking about to a degree as well. And that you can deliver some things... Probably the difficulty is knowing the problem is there and getting in early to fix it up. Very often you don't hear about the problems. Again, it's getting round and talking to people.

The difficulty of reversing the Government's mistrust of irrigators was in turn lessened significantly by irrigators choosing people to lead them in the LWMP programme (i.e. their representatives on the CWGs) who mostly were not linked with the SRIDC. Mr Martin described this transition as follows:

> The SRIDC tended to be the older irrigators that had been around agri-politics for a long time... The younger irrigators in the Berriquin, Wakool, Deniboota and Denimein planning

working groups were probably in their early 30s... So they were
the sons, a generation down, which I think was good because they
didn't come with the same baggage, if you like, from prior SRIDC
debates. They... came with a fairly open mind about the
Department and how it could do things.

The challenge facing this new generation of community leaders he described as
follows:

> All the irrigators weren't, in my view, convinced that the
> community could actually do it. Some of them were saying to us
> at that stage 'You go away and do it and tell us what we've got to
> do'. But a number of irrigators were championing the community
> involvement. There wasn't a lot of them to start with, but there
> was a growing groundswell. They had some strength and they had
> a fairly good argument that turned the views of some of the other
> irrigators anyway. There wasn't a full agreement, to start with,
> that they wanted actually to participate. Some of them had to be
> brought along... In Wakool and Denimein and Deniboota, some
> of the younger irrigators out there had some trouble convincing
> the older irrigators that participation was the way to go.

Pursuing community ownership

It seems that building the trust of the wider community in the authenticity of
the Government's offer of a collaborative partnership to address the watertable
related problems followed to a substantial extent from Mr Martin's active
commitment to the concept of 'community ownership'. Mr Stewart acknowledged this commitment as follows:

> I'll take my hat off to Government here. Government certainly
> had a concept which they wished to put into place. And that
> concept was community ownership of the Land and Water
> Management Plans. It was very clear to me when speaking to
> people like Warren Martin that certainly there'd be boundaries
> around what would go into these plans. There'd be Government
> policies and other constraints, but by and large you had a blank
> sheet of paper. And local community people – because they had
> to live in that environment and deal with its problems – were seen
> as the best people to come up with workable solutions.

From the commitment to community ownership followed the decision by
Government to appoint Mr Stewart as an independent Program Coordinator
for the LWMP programme. Mr Martin explained this step as follows:

> I saw it was essential to have someone in the [region] on-site...
> [A]ntagonism management and trust building were important

issues. My view was that we needed an independent person. We didn't want a Departmental person.

Mr Stewart took up this position in early 1992. Despite the good intentions on the part of Government, its lack of consultation with the CWGs about the appointment caused them concern that the commitment to community ownership of the process had been short-lived. Geoff McLeod – with the Government's agriculture department (then called NSW Agriculture) during the plan development phase of the LWMP programme, and Murray Irrigation's Environmental Manager at the time of interviewing – explained that the unilateral appointment made the CWGs wary that 'DWR [was] trying to run the show again'. Mr Stewart recalled, as follows, the consequent mistrust of him at the first CWG meeting he attended (with the Berriquin CWG):

> You could have cut the atmosphere with a knife… It was a difficult meeting for me. My view was that … if they didn't like what I had to offer then, well, that's the way life goes sometimes and I'll walk away. If they thought I had something to offer then that would dawn upon them and the relationship would start to develop.

Faced with this mistrust, he decided not to force himself onto the CWGs:

> I never pushed myself on to any of the Working Groups, ever. I deliberately waited to be invited. And I didn't get initial invitations, by the way. It wasn't a case of me just saying 'I'm the Planning Coordinator now for all you guys, and I expect to come to all your meetings'. They discussed it among themselves and I was invited initially to a meeting. And then it didn't take very long for them to say I should come to all their meetings.

A further strategy, instigated by Mr Martin, for establishing the independence of Mr Stewart from the Government was to accommodate him and his small team of staff away from the Government office premises. Aside from preserving his independence from the Government, Mr Stewart was careful to ensure that he protected it too from the various other sectional interests involved in the programme. He explained:

> That way I believed I could make sure that all stakeholder interests could be accommodated without me being seen as siding with any of them. I didn't side with any of them either. I never had one vote at any of the meetings, ever.

He saw that this required him to 'drive the process … in a fair kind of way without trying to impose your own views – what you're not looking for is content that *you* believe in; what you're trying to do is have a process that gets content that *they* believe in'. This role of driving the process was typically pursued through running 'workshop sessions' during CWG meetings –

although always in deference to the CWG chairperson. Mr. Stewart elaborated as follows on how he did this while maintaining CWG ownership of the ideas arising from these sessions:

> Just because of my exposure to a greater range of things, I was in a position to answer questions or give opinions. But I never used to operate in that way. I would always try to seek the opinions and views of the other people there. And nine times out of ten what you were thinking would come from someone else in any event. But then they had ownership of it.

In this way, the CWGs incrementally developed trust that the Government was respecting them as collaborators within the LWMP programme. Nevertheless, their own capacity to collaborate effectively depended crucially on their internal cohesion. Asked whether there was mistrust initially *within* the CWGs, Mr Stewart responded 'Yes, of course... Some people came in there with a bit of baggage, with a reputation for being this, that or the other thing'. The challenge of establishing trust within CWGs was probably greatest in the case of the Cadell LWMP District, which encompassed Deniboota Irrigation District as well as an area known as East Cadell, which contained private irrigation schemes as well as extensive dryland areas. Bill Anderson – who represented the latter area on the Cadell CWG and was representing it on the CIG at the time of interviewing – explained 'there has been a fair amount of feeling between the two areas', particularly because private irrigators in East Cadell believed that over the years Deniboota irrigators had won various concessions from Government at their expense. It was clearly important for a single CWG to represent the whole of the Cadell district since it formed a natural groundwater catchment – meaning that Deniboota irrigators would be unable to address their watertable related problems effectively without cooperation from East Cadell landholders.

Mr Graham, from Deniboota, suggested that success in encouraging East Cadell farmers to join the CWG was attributable to the Deniboota members of the CWG being a generation younger than the older Deniboota farmers and that East Cadell farmers would associate more directly with their 'feeling' in respect of Deniboota irrigators. He characterized the Deniboota members accordingly as 'sons of current property owners, idealistic, who presented no challenge to anyone. Nevertheless, we were old enough to represent the future and have our ideas respected'. Mr Anderson agreed with Mr Graham's interpretation of events and went on to observe that Jamie Hearn, who had been Chairperson of the Cadell CWG:

> was one of the greatest things in building bridges between East and West Cadell. Because he came from West Cadell, from Deniboota, but he showed an equal concern for those who lived in East Cadell.

Even so, it took genuine leadership for Mr Anderson and other

East Cadell farmers to agree to join the CWG. Mr Anderson remembered that '[I]t was hard at the start. I think a lot of people at the outset felt betrayed that we got involved'.

Within the CWGs it was understood that decisions would not be owned by all members unless an atmosphere of trust and respect among members existed that encouraged everyone to engage in a deliberative process of frankly airing their beliefs and values. Mr Stewart recalled:

> Someone said to me they'd remembered as important me saying 'There's no wrongs and rights, just differing opinions'. It was just something off the top of my head at the time. But it kind of settles people down and it generates the right atmosphere for people to put forward their points of view. The Working Group in Cadell was just terrific... They had the capacity to debate issues with a whole range of views in the room, but without acrimony.

Mr Liphuyzen observed similarly that:

> People have different opinions and you've got to let everyone express their opinions... so that you get that other view. Otherwise you'll be too blinkered in your approach... We did have one or two members at different times that were sticking on an issue and wouldn't change off it and were getting the rest of the group's backs up. But most of the time I think it worked pretty well.

Nevertheless, it was clear that ownership of the LWMPs by the CWGs would not in itself guarantee ownership by their respective communities. Consequently, each of the CWGs devised a strategy for engaging the inclusive participation of their respective communities in the LWMP programme. John Lacy – an agricultural extension officer with NSW Agriculture when interviewed, and previously a member of the Berriquin CWG – recalled that the CWG originally considered holding occasional large public meetings for the purpose of broadening community participation. However, his extension experience had taught him the advantages of small-group deliberative processes for achieving changes in farmer behaviour. He observed that:

> The big benefit of discussion groups is that it allows farmers to learn off each other and it allows farmers to give feedback. Farmers are looked on as being equals to the facilitator. It's just a great learning process.

Mr Lacy argued successfully that this approach to involving farmers should be adopted by the Berriquin CWG. The Berriquin District was accordingly divided up by the CWG into the localities within which small-group meetings would be convened. The other CWGs saw merit in this strategy and chose independently to follow similar strategies. Mr Liphuyzen commented on the effectiveness of this strategy in the Denimein District as follows:

> Smaller groups offer people much more of a hands-on involvement. They are much more at ease to comment on what they think of something. If you just had one regional meeting, you'd get people who always want to hear their own voice and also a lot of people that just sit and say nothing and have no input. So the smaller meetings were a good part of the process. If we came up with something that wasn't acceptable, I think we would have been told straight away.

Each of the three Berriquin farmers interviewed made similar comments. For instance, one of them said:

> There's only the odd one that gets up at a big public meeting. I think people feel far more comfortable speaking with their neighbours just in the local area than they do standing up at the town hall.

A further feature of the locality meetings that a number of those interviewed indicated was vital for their effectiveness in gaining ownership of the meeting outcomes by the participants was that the responsibility for chairing the meetings, presenting technical information and leading discussions was largely taken on by CWG members living in those localities. Mr Lahy said this strategy was instrumental in gaining trust from the wider farming community that the consultation process was genuine and that the information provided to them could be trusted.

Government–community collaboration in LWMP development

Ownership by the Government of the LWMP programme and the resulting plans was clearly critical also, especially given that it was providing resources to support development of the plans and looking to contribute considerable funds toward their implementation. Consequently, it had a legitimate interest in ensuring that plan development was technically sound. This was acknowledged in Mr Stewart's comment that:

> I saw there'd need to be a process which engaged the community but also had strong technical support to it as well. And the two were interactive all the way through... So there was a sort of marriage of farming common sense and aspirations with the technical side of things.

Nevertheless, the marriage was not always an easy one. For instance, some of the CWGs believed strongly that the Government's commitment to community ownership of the planning process meant that they should be given a real say in how the funds provided by the MDBC for technical studies were used. They were wary that the DWR would dominate these kinds of decisions by virtue of being the recipient of those funds, and consequently retain 'in-house' more of the technical programme than justified by its capacity to complete tasks proficiently on schedule. According to Mr Stewart, 'at the start the Department said "Yeah, it's all contestable. It is alright if you go out into the marketplace". But that only lasted until the crunch time came'. He observed that it was a case of:

> The Golden Rule applies: He who has the gold makes the rules...
> When an external source of funds comes up, such as LWMP
> money, the temptation is to not use it entirely on the purpose for
> which it was given. Thus sometimes tenuous connections were
> made between the LWMPs and what people were doing in the
> Department, in order to justify paying Departmental staff salaries
> from that bucket of money... and that did happen to some extent.

Mr Stewart attributed this problem of CWG dissatisfaction with collaboration by Government regarding the use of programme resources to a lack of appropriate experience and skills on the part of key Government staff in the region. He recalled:

> There was a commitment [from government staff in the region],
> that's one thing. You may have a commitment to marry, but you
> may still end up divorced. No, they didn't have the skills...
> [S]aying it will work isn't enough to make it work. The people
> who are involved have to make it work.

However, Mr Martin indicated as follows that the problem may also have been partly due to paternalistic attitudes lingering at the regional level in DWR:

> When the LWMPs started, the region still at that stage regarded
> the irrigation areas and districts as their responsibility to a degree
> because the privatization hadn't occurred... Some of the
> management people in the region didn't like it at all, having the
> irrigators telling them what to do.

Another reason for the problem was lack of appreciation by CWG members of the complexity of some of the technical issues. As Mr Martin observed: 'The community will always think that you can do modelling in about a tenth of the time that you can actually do it in'. He went on to comment that this misunderstanding lessened as the CWGs became more aware of the complexities involved: 'I think there is now a better understanding of how difficult it is in a lot of these exercises to actually undertake technical studies, and get answers, and actually have to make decisions'.

Government–community collaboration in implementing the LWMPs

The LWMPs developed were, after a process of negotiation, ultimately agreed to by the communities of the four LWMP Districts, as well as by the Government. Ownership of the plans by the various District communities was demonstrated, in the words of Mr Stewart, by:

> the overwhelming support the plans got at the final stage. Every plan had a large community meeting at the end to see if the plan was supported or not. And they turned up in their droves. They gave a tick to what their Working Group had done.

What had been agreed between the District communities and the Government was formalized in a Heads of Agreement, as mentioned previously. Mr Ball remarked that this document is valued by the communities, as well as by MIL as the designated implementation authority for the LWMPs, as providing them with greater trust that Government will deliver on its side of the LWMP implementation programme than they would have taken away from promises backed only by handshakes. Mr Stewart observed likewise that 'I think that one of the real strengths of the LWMPs is the extent to which obligations were stitched up in a 'contractual' sense'.

By the same token, signing the Heads of Agreement represented a significant concession from the communities of the LWMP Districts. When asked about the strengths of the LWMP programme, Ros Chivers, then an officer in the head office of the DLWC, replied:

> I think the fact that there are, for want of a better word, contractual arrangements in place that require landholders and Murray Irrigation to actually do what they agreed they would do, so that we do get on-ground change. Without those sorts of contractual arrangements, we are finding that there is very little sustained on-ground change in other areas of the State. In other areas maybe $A100,000 is handed out for certain work to be done, but it's not necessarily the case that the work is carried out or maintained. Because there is no monitoring and evaluation, nor any contractual arrangement to say 'If you don't do it, then we will penalize you'.

Warren Musgrave, who was Chairperson of the LWMPAT when interviewed, remarked similarly that community–government collaboration process followed in the LWMP programme had:

> been a success in the sense that you have a contractually-based partnership arrangement between government and a community group for a plan where the costs are shared between the two partners... This to my mind is a significant breakthrough in resource management in Australia, to give that degree of discipline

and formality of agreement between the parties. And to get to the point of actually having done it is a fantastic achievement... Now I don't think that a top-down approach would get you that far. Except perhaps with significantly greater incentives.

This last sentence indicates that the greater trust in the plans and Government that the communities gained as a result of participating in the programme had a tangible economic impact in so far as it made them more amenable to cooperating voluntarily with Government – thereby reducing the transaction costs of inducing them to do so. The following observation from Mr Martin demonstrates the vital contribution that the leadership of the District communities, namely the CWGs, and the trust that was engendered in them through the community participation process, made to realizing this outcome:

You've got to give the credit for the success probably to the Working Groups and the Chairs who ran them... It wasn't all pats on the back from the community people for the LWMPs. Gerard Lahy often told me 'I don't know why I'm doing this. I'm getting more abuse out of this than doing other things. I could be away just managing my farm'... He actually drove the community through some of the changes. When he took back to his community the funding negotiation outcomes, he had some trouble getting their agreement to them... [He] had to battle to get endorsement because some of the community were saying 'No, Government should be paying more'.

In fact, this ownership by the CWGs of the plans they had developed caused considerable tension when it became apparent to them that the Government intended MIL, once the privatization had proceeded, to become responsible for implementing the four LWMPs. As Mr Baxter, who was to become the first Chairperson of Murray Irrigation, recalled:

There was no doubt that the four individual CWGs developed a fair bit of ownership of what they were doing and desired to be themselves responsible for implementing the LWMPs. It was like 'It's our plan and we'll implement it ourselves, thank you very much'. But they would never have been incorporated bodies, and that would have presented problems with managing the Government funds and so forth. And Murray Irrigation was going to be the entity that held the Supply License, the Operating License and the Pollution Control License. And a condition of those licenses was successful implementation of the LWMPs. It's not that we didn't trust those blokes, but we reckoned we'd need to have our foot on it. So a reasonably tense situation developed...

Mr Martin elaborated upon this account as follows:

> [I]n the end Kelvin Baxter became a very strong advocate and had to go and sell the new company as the implementer. And he managed to sell it. But the Board[1] itself wasn't necessarily fully trusted. People downstream in Deniboota and Wakool saw the Board as looking after Berriquin and not looking after them.

Eventually a compromise involving a nested organizational system was negotiated. According to Mr Baxter:

> [It] was resolved in a common-sense way... [W]e ended up with the LWMPs all under the control of Murray Irrigation. And I say that only in an institutional sort of way. The framework still gave the CIGs plenty of room for local autonomy regarding local decisions about what was best for their area and their plans. Under the framework Murray Irrigation was responsible for the CIGs' actions. We had to ensure that what they did in their plan areas was in the best interests of us complying with our licenses. Provided our aims were being satisfied there, they were, and still are, given a lot of latitude in how they implement the broad objectives of the LWMPs.

This nested arrangement seems to have worked out reasonably well. For instance, Mr Liphuyzen remarked that a number of issues had led the Denimein CIG to:

> sort of come to loggerheads with Murray Irrigation. But I suppose Geoff McLeod, Murray Irrigation's Environmental Manager, also has got to answer to the CIGs for the other LWMPs. He's also got to answer back to Murray Irrigation. So when we try to push something through, we've got to have something that is workable and that we can all live with. So there has been a bit of compromise there. And Geoff's also got to ensure that the LWMPs are acceptable to LWMPAT as well. Whoever we had as the implementing body would have had the same onus on them. We've been happy enough with Murray Irrigation.

This account meshes well with Mr McLeod's description of Murray Irrigation's experience with the arrangement:

> From time to time, there has been inconsistency between the [MIL] Board's desires and the desires of the CIGs. But I think that, in almost all cases, the differences have all been adequately resolved, albeit with a bit of pain. With some issues, I guess, the groups have wanted to take a more 'softly, softly' approach to change. Individuals on the groups of course are going to be directly affected by some of that change. Obviously, they can

influence the decisions that are made in their groups. Whereas the Board has a broader responsibility.

Common property management of community compliance with the LWMPs

The Heads of Agreement had the effect of decentralizing to MIL the task of ensuring that farmers within each of the four Districts comply with their collective on-farm obligations under their respective LWMPs. Consistent with the concept of organizational nesting, this common property regime was left considerable autonomy as to how this might be achieved. The LWMP programme in this way came also to satisfy Ostrom's (1990, p90) seventh design principle for long-enduring regimes of common property: 'The rights of appropriators to devise their own institutions are not challenged by external governmental authorities'.

Mr McLeod characterized the strategy MIL Irrigation applied in ensuring on-farm compliance with the LWMPs as follows:

> Our approach has been, first, education, second, encourage by incentives, third, make them aware that there are sticks in the cupboard and, fourth, you pull the stick out and use it. We hope that we don't have to get to the last stage. As a generalization, we often see that people only do the wrong thing because they don't understand the impacts of what they are doing. We focus first on increasing landholders' awareness of the impact of their actions, or how they might change their actions to benefit others as well as themselves. Murray Irrigation has got the ultimate stick of being able to turn someone's water off. We seek to use that as sparingly as possible... But there are individuals who will always try and get around us. And anyone who does, by stealing water for example, is hit pretty hard. Their wheels are locked, and their irrigation allocations are debited. For farmers who grow rice on unsuitable soils, there are water penalties applied to them.

The hope was that co-ownership by irrigators of the regime responsible for intervening to ensure LWMP implementation, together with the dependence of this common-property regime and themselves on successful implementation, would make them more prepared to cooperate with interventions than if it were the Government, which historically they had mistrusted, that was intervening. Indeed, this hope appears from the comments of key informants to have materialized in significant degree. For instance, Tony McGlynn, a senior officer in the head office of the DLWC at the time of interviewing, judged that locating responsibility for enforcing implementation of the LWMPs with MIL had been 'very important in getting real change on farms. You wouldn't be able to get it out of Government. It would be a 'dig in' situation'. Consistent with this view, one of the Berriquin farmers interviewed said 'I think now, as Murray Irrigation's shareholders, we can see that it has to take more responsibility for environmental management and that they've got to do something'.

It seems also that irrigators are becoming aware that Murray Irrigation's responsibility for enforcing implementation has put the region's irrigation community in the position of being able to establish a trustworthy environmental reputation for itself rather than merely attempt to avoid a bad reputation. One farmer interviewed remarked along these lines that:

> I personally feel it's better with Murray Irrigation doing it [making and enforcing the rules]. And it demonstrates to the Government that we are serious and that we are trying. It's no longer the Government chasing us around and saying 'You're not doing the right thing'... If we can collectively show through Murray Irrigation that we are trying, and that we're not going to tolerate people that do the wrong things, it must help us collectively. It's important that we look like we're trying to proceed down the right path, because there's a lot of negative feeling about irrigators.

Moreover, the comments received indicate considerable confidence that MIL is more committed and successful in its attempts to expedite LWMP implementation by farmers than would be the case if Government were the responsible entity. Mr Jacob, a consultant involved in the LWMP programme, commented for example that:

> [Y]ou now have a very environmentally-responsible irrigation entity... compared with when the irrigation schemes were under government ownership... We've been surprised by how quickly the private entity in this case has picked up the resource management role.

Sandy Robinson, from the Murray Darling Basin Commission, observed similarly from her experience with the LWMP programme that 'it's interesting that once you've got things down to an arrangement, communities tend to be tougher on themselves than they'll let government be with them'. Likewise, Mr Hearn thought that MIL had achieved far more in implementing the LWMPs than would be the case if the Government were still responsible. The company had introduced some tough policies in support of the LWMPs, which he believed would have been beyond the political will of Government to introduce effectively. He claimed that around 15–20 per cent of farmers were upset by these policies.

Nevertheless, MIL cannot take for granted that the cooperation from most farmers it enjoyed originally will continue. Ms Robinson recalled confronting people in the company with this challenge by asking them 'How do you not become "those bastards in town" as opposed to "those bastards in Sydney"?' Mr McLeod acknowledged that maintaining the trust and cooperation of farmers would depend on the company continuing to engage their inclusive participation in its policy making deliberations. He claimed accordingly that:

> The company does go out of its way to listen to what people are saying, not only to be seen doing it. When developing major policies we have on each occasion set up consultative committees of local landholders to develop those policies. Our Directors are democratically elected, so I guess they are very much aware that if they ignore the views of their constituency they may not be on the Board the next time around.

In addition, as observed by Mr Baxter, irrigators have also kept MIL accountable since privatization through the SRIDC, which in that time has actively pursued a new 'role of watchdog for the shareholders in respect of how Murray Irrigation operates'. Due to these democratic checks and balances, a considerable degree of flexibility typically has been built into MIL's environmental policies in order to satisfy local norms of fairness.

A key issue concerns the extent to which the status of irrigators as co-owners of the governance regime has made them more likely to help it meet its LWMP implementation obligations by applying to one another the kinds of informal social sanctions that they use in other contexts to informally encourage adherence to local customs or norms. According to Mr Baxter, this new-found status has indeed made them:

> more likely to take action against fellow farmers [who exceed their rights to extract water from the irrigation supply channels] than they were before. Previously it was seen as the Government's water, and it was a bit of a sport trying to rip the Government off. But when it's your own system, then they are ripping you off.

However, it seems at this relatively early stage of the LWMP implementation process that any sanctioning by farmers in respect of one another's adoption of LWMP measures that does occur is mostly one-to-one through casually proffered admiration or information. For instance, one of the Berriquin farmers interviewed commented:

> I don't encourage other farmers. But if someone says 'You've done that. What do you reckon about that?', then I'm very happy to say 'We've done these things and this worked and that hasn't worked'. No, we don't go around telling people what they should or shouldn't be doing.

He added:

> I don't think you are looked upon badly [by other farmers] if you don't do the things in the LWMP, because it's understood that it costs a lot of money to do it and so you might not be able to afford

to do it… But if you do a good job on your farm I think people will think 'He's done a good job on his farm'. So perhaps that is a social kind of encouragement to follow the LWMP on your farm.

Another farmer responded similarly when asked whether he thought there was social pressure on farmers to adopt LWMP measures: 'No, not at this stage. You get some pretty negative press… But you really don't take an awful lot of notice of that'. Nevertheless, the following anecdote from Mr Liphuyzen indicates that farmers can be prepared to exert peer pressure on one another in instances where there is an open lack of support for the LWMP programme that they feel is unjustified:

> We've had one or two people in the community that weren't overly enthused about the [Denimein] LWMP… And I've actually seen a classic case of social pressure down at the pub here. One of them started going on about how he didn't like this and he didn't like that. Three other people turned around and pounced on him and made him shut up. He's actually in the process of doing a farm plan now, and moving ahead too.

Mr Liphuyzen suggested as follows that peer pressure among farmers to adopt LWMP measures would strengthen with their increasing awareness of the costs of not doing so for the environment and for the reputation of the region's irrigation industry: 'As people become more aware, they will say "Look at that fella there. He's ripping all his trees out. He shouldn't be doing that"'. Another reason why peer pressure among farmers to adopt LWMP measures may strengthen with time was suggested by one of the farmers interviewed: 'As more and more farmers take it up, I think greater pressure will be brought to bear on the ones that aren't doing it'. This possibility is consistent with Mr Hearn's comment that:

> The plan is very much alive in people's minds. There is lots of 'looking over the fence' to see what other farmers have done. It's like a 'domino effect'. One farmer's uptake of LWMP practices leads others to follow suit.

To the extent that peer pressure among farmers does strengthen with time, it seems likely that CIG members will find themselves with an important role in mediating this social process. As Mr Hearn remarked, CIG members are normally the focus of day-to-day feedback from farmers about the LWMPs, including gossip regarding the activities of particular farmers. As Knox and Meinzen-Dick (2001) have observed from international experience, it is not uncommon for members of local communities to avoid the risk of endangering relationships with neighbours that sanctioning them directly may involve. In farming communities, each relationship can constitute a vital portion of the social capital available to an individual for meeting needs such as help with emergencies and companionship. As Mr Stewart observed, '[I]n the country…

if you alienate your neighbour you can't just go a hundred metres and find another one. That's it, you're boxed in'.

Key lessons

The case study of the LWMP programme confirmed that trust has been pivotal in influencing farmers' cooperation within this programme. Moreover, it showed that the trust of farmers affecting their cooperation within the programme is multi-faceted. Thus, the cooperation of individual farmers within the programme has been affected by their trust in, at least: the Government's commitment to a collaborative planning and implementation approach; other farmers' commitment to comply with their LWMP obligations; the authenticity of the process of community participation; and in their community-based organizations (MIL and their District's CIG) not allowing their own interests to sideline the interests of the farmers and other community members they claim to represent.

A range of structural variables were found to affect these facets of farmers' trust. For instance, particular reasons were identified for the LWMP programme's history of mutual antagonism and mistrust between the region's irrigators and the Government. These reasons included: paternalistic attitudes of Government staff; divergent interests of farmers and the Government (e.g. regarding whether maintenance of employment levels in running the irrigation scheme should be an objective of its governance); and the confrontational nature of irrigators' leadership in the past.

The key role that leadership played in allowing the LWMP programme to circumvent 'lock in' of Government staff and irrigators to the mistrusting mental models inherited from their history of mutual antagonism was also highlighted. Aspects of governmental leadership found to be important in gaining farmers' trust in this case included: the senior position held by the person who became primarily responsible for the Government's leadership; this leader's willingness and capacity to 'champion' the programme beyond his own department to other critical agencies including Treasury; and this leader's willingness and capacity to build personal relationships with farmer leaders and to adopt a 'hands-on' leadership style. The aspect of farmer leadership identified as particularly important in this case was the selection by farmers of a younger generation of leaders relatively free of the 'baggage' associated with prior Government-irrigator conflicts, and also naturally more inclined to embrace the longer-term perspective required to effectively deal with their Districts' salinity and waterlogging problems.

The importance of a number of structural variables targeted by the LWMP programme in its efforts to overcome irrigators' longstanding lack of trust in Government-initiated programmes for their sector was also confirmed by the case study. One such variable relates to where responsibility for regional coordination of the programme was assigned. In this case, the responsibility was assigned to a Program Coordinator who was: independent of both the Government and the District communities; given office accommodation away from Government offices and existing community organizations; committed to the collaborative vision; and who had considerable experience and skills with which to motivate the District communities and Government towards the vision's fruition. Organizing the programme's strategy for community participation along the lines of small discussion groups convened at places convenient for farmers was also found to be a key structural factor in gaining their trust.

The case study also confirmed the essential contribution that formally institutionalizing the commitments by the community and the Government in respect of implementing the LWMPs – through the Heads of Agreement and associated licensing arrangements – made to establishing the high level of trust between them needed for the commitments to be converted into collective action rather than be undermined by free riding. In addition, it found that farmers are more prepared to trust MIL to implement the on-farm elements of the LWMPs than they would the Government, and consequently that they are more prepared to cooperate with the policies in place for ensuring on-farm compliance as a result of the responsibility for these policies having been decentralized to MIL. Indeed, decentralization of this authority to MIL appears to have resulted in markedly stronger policies being introduced in support of on-farm implementation than the Government would have found politically feasible to introduce.

Finally, the possibility that the decentralization of authority to MIL, a common property regime, would lead farmers – as co-owners of that regime – to take a more active role in sanctioning one another's on-farm LWMP implementation was also explored in the case study. Any such effect appeared weak at the time of interviewing, with 'first party' sanctioning of this kind limited mainly to gestures of social approval to farmers who have made progress with on-farm implementation. Nevertheless, there was an expectation among some of the farmers and farmer leaders interviewed that their peers would become more active in sanctioning one another's compliance once the deadlines for meeting the district level on-farm adoption targets loom closer, and as the momentum of on-farm adoption builds and non-complying farmers become fewer and more noticeable.

Part IV

Grounding the Collaborative Vision

7

Rethinking Policy, Practice and Research

The problem addressed in this book concerns the mostly disappointing record to date of attempts to convert collaborative environmental management from vision to practice. The urgency of gaining knowledge of how to pursue this vision more successfully has come to be recognized in recent years. Adaptive management – where collaborative efforts are regarded as institutional experiments to be learned from in designing subsequent efforts – is becoming regarded widely (outside mainstream economics at least) as the appropriate strategy for obtaining this knowledge given the complexity and diversity of the social and natural systems that are involved. Nevertheless, there is a need for theory to guide the choice of experiments and to structure the learning that occurs once the choices are made.

In previous chapters we have sought to meet this need and illustrate how the theory presented applies to, and can be elaborated by, actual experiences with collaborative environmental management. The focus in this chapter turns to the implications of what we have learned along the way for policy makers, practitioners and researchers concerned with establishing the potential of the collaborative vision and bringing that potential to fruition across a wide diversity of contexts. The implications for policy makers and practitioners are explored first, after which a strategy for researchers in this area to follow is proposed. Consistent with this broad strategy, a more targeted strategy is outlined for applying empirically the framework for cost effectiveness analysis of complex institutional choices that was presented in Chapter 4. The chapter closes with some brief comments regarding the value of such research in giving governments the confidence they need to shift from what mostly remain, at best, half-hearted efforts to realize the collaborative vision to the bold, innovative and systematic efforts that are necessary for success in this direction.

Implications for the policy and practice of collaborative environmental management

The experiences of collaborative environmental and natural resource management reviewed in the previous two chapters indicate that the prediction from mainstream, comparative static economics – that zero voluntary cooperation is inevitable within large-group commons problems – is too pessimistic. The developments of rational choice collective action theory reviewed in Chapter 3 – which explain how large-group voluntary cooperation can emerge and grow under supportive conditions through increasing return dynamics involving trust and reciprocity – provide a more instructive and accurate, albeit less precise, explanation of the behaviour observed.

Consistent with these developments in collective action theory, the case study of the Murray LWMP programme presented in Chapter 6 illustrated the positive effect of trust building between collaborators on their preparedness to spontaneously initiate and reciprocate cooperation with one another. It demonstrated not only how path dependency of the mental models that collaborators use to assess each other's trustworthiness arises from their history of prior interactions, but also how collaboration as a democratic process of deliberation helped collaborators to avoid the associated trap of lock-in to mental models that changes in their circumstances – including the trustworthiness of others – make adaptively inefficient.

Implications of these findings for ongoing efforts by policy makers and practitioners to realize the collaborative vision for environmental management are considered in this section. After a general review of key implications, the discussion turns to particular challenges and opportunities in respect of developing the capacities needed within both governments and communities for them to help realize the vision.

Three key lessons

The empirical evidence in support of the 'new generation' rational choice theory of collective action suggests three key lessons relevant to bringing the collaborative vision for environmental management to fruition. The first of these is that this vision is not a hallucination despite the widespread frustration that its pursuit since the 1980s has caused. The vision could be dismissed as a hallucination if it were not possible to provide a plausible theoretical explanation of how it might be realized in actual contexts of environmental management. Indeed, this was the situation when the only theory of collective action was the mainstream, comparative static theory. This theory predicts zero voluntary cooperation within a large group, even if group members collaborate so successfully that they come to agree unanimously that they should cooperate in a certain way.

A second key lesson suggested by the experiences reviewed, and particularly by the case study reported in the previous chapter, concerns the difficulty that government officers and community members face in comprehending the collaborative vision through the lens of mental models adapted to the Progressive vision. As exemplified by comparative static models of collective action, these mental models account systematically for diminishing-return (negative-feedback) aspects of dynamic processes but not the increasing-return (positive-feedback) aspects through which large-group voluntary cooperation can possibly emerge. For those with mental models of this kind, the proposition that collaboration can instigate and strengthen large-group voluntary cooperation is simply not tenable. The collaborative vision will therefore at best be afforded 'lip service' by governmental and non-governmental stakeholders whose mental models remain rooted in the Progressive world view.

The third key lesson is that facilitating escape from lock-in to Progressive mental models requires enlightened and committed leadership. It is not sufficient for leaders to merely announce that the Progressive vision for environmental management is no longer appropriate and that it should be replaced by a collaborative vision. It is a mistake commonly made by leaders to underestimate the difficulty of translating their own visions into visions that are shared by those they seek to lead (Kotter, 1995). According to Senge (1990, p206), a 'shared vision is a vision that many people are truly committed to, because it reflects their own personal vision'. As Kotter (1995) argued, people will not commit to a new vision until they become convinced that the previous vision has become inadequate *and* that following the new one would yield a superior result.

Leading people to commit to a new vision is typically challenging as a result of the beliefs or mental models selected by the existing vision having become locked in. The more that one's existing human and social capital is adapted to the mental models currently held by others, the greater is the motivation to discourage others from committing to a new vision and thus changing to a new set of mental models consonant with this vision. In addition, existing institutions are the result of – and thus reinforce – existing mental models.

Moreover, mental models constitute a vital component of human self-identity. Harrison (1997, p261) remarked accordingly that changing peoples' mental models is difficult 'because it requires the capacity for objective introspection and attribution to internal factors that touch on the most sensitive questions of self-image and respect'. Consequently, '[i]ndividuals will often accept intellectual arguments, understand their need to change, and express commitment to changing, but then resort to what is familiar' (Lindsay, 2000, p283). This points to the importance of leading people towards the collaborative vision through processes of deliberative discourse, since mental models often exist below the level of awareness where they result in beliefs or assumptions becoming accepted mistakenly as facts. Senge (1990, p203) argued accordingly that '[u]ntil prevailing assumptions are brought into the open, there is no reason to expect mental models to change'. Mental models regarding the (un)trustworthiness of the parties one is expected to collaborate with can be locked in particularly deeply. As Wondolleck and Yaffee (2000, p58) remarked in relation to natural resource management: 'A general sense of wariness and skepticism frequently pervades all sides of the collaboration equation due to past interactions, stereotypes, and a societal context that breeds mistrust'.

Challenges in developing governmental capacities to promote collaboration

One of the major obstacles to gaining the commitment of government officers to the collaborative vision for environmental governance derives from mental models adapted to the Progressive vision disregarding the increasing returns associated with collaboration, and thereby portraying attempts at large-group cooperation as inevitably involving 'win–lose' interactions. Such models of large-group collective action predict that contributions to providing a collective good will simply become free rides for non-contributing parties. That is, those who contribute through collaborating are forecast to lose by the same amount in total that free riders win.

The collaborative vision requires government officers to cooperate in providing a new system of governance by decentralizing to, or sharing with, communities some of the responsibilities and rights that traditionally have been theirs. However, the win–lose mental models associated with this vision lead these officers to expect that cooperating in this way will mean a loss for themselves and a corresponding win for the communities involved. Hence, Koontz et al (2004, p177) found from their case studies of collaborative environmental management in the US that 'individuals invested in bureaucratic structures and processes may view collaborative environmental management as a threat'. They may fear for instance that their cooperation will result in the agencies employing them being restructured and/or down-sized, thereby threatening their job security (Knox and Meinzen-Dick, 2001).

Officers may also resist cooperating within government–community collaboration programmes because of an expectation that the outcome for them of successful collaboration would be reduced job status or satisfaction. For instance, Koontz et al (2004, p177) found that 'because some individuals and agencies may be uncomfortable if they are not fully in control, they may resist or be antagonistic to collaboration'. Wondolleck and Yaffee (2000, p61) reported an officer in a natural resources management agency as saying that collaboration meets obstacles because it has 'disrupted the comfort level that some employees have developed over the years'. Indeed, adapting successfully to the collaborative vision does often require officers to obtain new skills and/or agencies to change their selection criteria for new staff. As observed by Selin and Chavez (1995, p189), '[m]anagers need new skills to move from the expert opinion role in traditional environmental management to an empowerment role as a mediator, catalyst, or broker in the new order'.

Government officers' fears that they will lose from supporting collaboration often exaggerate reality. This is the case when the fears are based on mental models that are biased against recognizing the interdependencies between government agencies and communities – interdependencies that offer possibilities of discovering win–win solutions that allay at least some of the downside of cooperating. This highlights a general need for leaders championing a new vision to remove obstacles to its successful pursuit (Kotter, 1995). For instance, fears that job status or satisfaction will decline if authentic collaboration proceeds may be headed off by proactively training staff in the requisite new skills and changing recruitment and promotion criteria to reward mastery and application of these skills. Where the culture of passive resistance to genuine collaboration is widespread within an agency, this resistance may be eroded more successfully if whole teams of staff are trained simultaneously. There may be fears too that greater collaboration with communities will increase workloads as well as stress levels. These can be overcome, first, by leaders ensuring that staff are resourced at levels appropriate to their new roles and, second, by reforming institutional arrangements – informal as well as formal – within and across agencies that present obstacles to collaborating with communities (Wondolleck and Yaffee, 2000). The obstacles in the US posed by existing bureaucratic rules and norms to effective engagement of government officers in collaboration environmental management were highlighted by Koontz et al (2004).

Nevertheless, narrow self-interest is often not the only reason for government officers baulking at committing themselves to the collaborative vision. They may have legitimate concerns that they do not know enough about the communities to which they are supposed to decentralize responsibilities to trust that fruitful collaboration is feasible. Knox and Meinzen-Dick (2001, p9) observed accordingly how:

> Without a track record of local people's capacity to manage resources, states are being asked to take a leap of faith in entrusting a fundamental source of wealth to those whose management capacity has not been well-tested or documented.

As discussed in Chapter 5, it can be possible for governments to surmount this obstacle by finding ways to build their trust in communities incrementally. Thus, '[g]overnments that are ... dubious of local people's capacity to assume control over resource management may find a gradual process of rights transfer more palatable or reassuring' (ibid, p19). This kind of strategy works through 'systematically planning for and creating short-term wins' (Kotter, 1995, p65), given that '[p]eople are more likely to change their attitudes and behavior when they see demonstrations of success' (Fairbanks, 2000, p279). However, bureaucracies often overlook the opportunities presented by instances of success for motivating their staff. A number of persons interviewed for the case study of the LWMP programme reported in Chapter 6 expressed frustration that opportunities for the NSW and Commonwealth Governments to celebrate across the Australian natural resources policy community the considerable successes of government–community collaboration in this programme had been largely neglected. A senior officer in the Murray Darling Basin Commission lamented:

> There is nobody marketing the achievements of [the LWMPs] ... Overall, my assessment was and still is that the Murray plans are the most comprehensive [collaborative natural resource management plans] that I've seen developed anywhere within Australia... One of my great frustrations is that the NSW Government, and to a smaller extent the Commonwealth, don't really appreciate how good those plans are.

Another challenge in gaining authentic commitment from governments to pursuing the collaborative vision can arise from their reluctance to invest in the process of adaptive management needed to cope with the complex institutional choices this pursuit entails. Jiggins and Röling (2002, p6) observed that politicians and government officers baulk at the cost of investing in the systems required to learn effectively from policy experiences, especially since even well-run adaptive management processes seldom lead 'conclusively [to the] cut-and-dried answers that politicians need'. These frustrations point to the importance of developing ways of learning more cost effectively from policy experimentation, and of better translating what is learnt into practical strategies for policy implementation.

The final obstacle in building governmental capacities for engaging effectively with collaborative programmes to be mentioned here arises from the brevity of the attention spans of many politicians relative to the time scales needed normally to succeed with programmes of this kind. This means that the policy and organizational contexts of many such programmes never remain stable enough for collaboration to launch, let alone sustain, the 'virtuous circles' needed to fuel the spontaneous emergence of trust and voluntary cooperation upon which realization of the collaborative vision ultimately depends (Huxham and Vangen, 2000a). Connor and Dovers (2004, p227) concluded accordingly that 'within bounds of suitability to the sustainability problem, the actual choice of institutional strategy ... matters less than the persistence of commitment to that strategy, resources, reiteration of efforts and maintenance of the policy regime'.

Challenges in developing community capacities to promote collaboration

states as sovereign players

Government agencies indeed have a 'unique and central role in guiding collaborative initiatives' since they 'are the only parties that have explicit authorities and responsibilities assigned to them under law' (Wondolleck and Yaffee, 2000, p213). As the case study of the LWMP programme reported in Chapter 6 highlighted, however, successful community–government collaboration can also depend heavily on community leadership that understands and is committed to the collaborative vision, and is trusted by its followers. The existence of such leadership ready-made cannot be taken for granted given the paternalism that has characterized governmental pursuit of the Progressive vision. Such paternalism restricts the chances for community members to develop their capacities for leadership of collaborative programmes. As illustrated by the case study of the Murray LWMP programme, the community leadership that does arise in such circumstances is often preoccupied with reacting to and opposing government, and thus may not possess the mental models, reputations or social networks best suited for proactively pursuing the collaborative vision. The key role that 'on the job training' within the LWMP programme, as provided informally by the Program Coordinator, played in preparing a new generation of community leaders to operate collaboratively – with each other, with their constituents, and with government – was also evident from the case study. For instance, Noel Graham explained in his interview that, although the members of the Cadell CWG were not given formal training in collaborative leadership skills, they did eventually acquire such skills by emulating the example set by the Program Coordinator in facilitating authentic dialogue and deliberation.

While fostering capable leadership can undoubtedly help move community members towards understanding and committing to the collaborative vision, the strength of history's grip on their mental models should not be underestimated. Some idea of how reluctantly history loosens its grip is given by Putnam's (1993) observation that contemporary differences in the self-governing capabilities of regional communities in Italy can be traced to a cultural split between the South and North of the country around the year 1100 (associated with the founding of the Norman Kingdom in the South and the communal republics in the North). Although he observed that nation-wide decentralization of governmental functions to the regions in the 1970s had already favourably affected the behaviour of politicians in the South – where regions inherited markedly lower self-governing capacities as a result of the Normans coming to govern much more hierarchically and paternalistically than did the republics – he concluded that the spread among citizens in the South of the reciprocity they need to govern themselves more self-reliantly will take appreciably longer to become apparent than in the North.

It is possible too that citizens may not have learned norms of reciprocity or have some moral objection to following them. Might obstacles of this kind be overcome through civic education? Axelrod (1984) observed that doubts about the morality of reciprocity partly explain the reluctance of citizens to use it as a norm in their interactions with one another. He noted that the Golden Rule – 'Do unto others as you would have them do unto you' – remains a dominant ethic in Western societies. This implies a norm of unconditional cooperation, since cooperation is what is wanted from others. Hence 'turning the other cheek' is considered virtuous, whereas reciprocating non-cooperation is not. However, turning one's cheek burdens the rest of the community in two ways. First, by leaving non-cooperative behaviour unpunished, the likelihood of others in the community encountering such behaviour is increased. Second, it transfers the task of reforming non-cooperative behaviour to the rest of the community. Hence, Axelrod reasoned that reciprocity is superior to unconditional cooperation as a foundation for morality, provided that the content of reciprocal actions accords with each community's moral code.

Axelrod argued accordingly for civic education regarding the advantages of reciprocity as a moral basis for individual behaviour within collective action problems. In the context of individual cases of collaborative environmental management, such as the Murray LWMP programme, this might appropriately be through group-based exercises which demonstrate to individuals how reciprocity can help to build spontaneous cooperation, and which also provide opportunities for them to discuss how sanctions can be applied consistently with local norms. Skills in applying such sanctions without endangering valued personal relationships might also be developed experientially through a process of this kind. However, for the broader scale it would seem more efficient to embed education of this kind within the mainstream educational system. Indeed, Ostrom (1998a, p18) argued in this spirit that:

> we need to translate our research findings on collective action
> into materials written for high school and undergraduate

students... It is ordinary persons and citizens who craft and sustain the workability of the institutions of everyday life. We owe an obligation to the next generation to carry forward the best of our knowledge about how individuals solve the multiplicity of social dilemmas – large and small – that they face.

A strategy for research into collaborative environmental management

As observed previously, adaptive management is becoming widely accepted as the appropriate strategy for acquiring the knowledge needed to cope with the complexity of translating the collaborative vision for environmental governance into practice within particular contexts. Until recently, however, the scope to rigorously apply adaptive management in pursuit of the collaborative vision has been limited by the lack of theory from which this endeavour might plausibly be launched. This obstacle would appear to be surmounted with the theoretical developments discussed in Chapters 3 and 4. Nevertheless, how should we proceed from here? If adaptive management involves treating policy initiatives as experiments to be learned from, what is the best way for us to learn from policy experiments in respect of collaborative environmental management?

Clearly, research has a vital role to play in facilitating the interpretation and exchange of feedback upon which depends the ability of communities and governments to learn from policy experiments in this domain. Seeking out, recording and organizing this feedback so that it can be drawn upon selectively to help design new generations of experiments would seem to be too demanding a project to thrust solely upon the people caught up in deciding and implementing particular policies. Rudd (2004, p121) observed accordingly that a challenge to effective adaptive management of fishery systems is that '[d]ecision-makers often have very little time to consider the implications of their decisions and they are often called on to make decisions in fields in which they have limited expertise'. This kind of challenge was also highlighted by Professor Warren Musgrave when asked, in his interview for the case study reported in the previous chapter, how effectively the NSW Government had learned from its experiences with collaborative natural resource management:

I get the impression that the capacity of government to articulate lessons learnt and to make generalizations about its experience is very limited. That's because of the demands on it, its lack of resources. Universities have an important role in this respect, in making generalizations and being reflective about experience. Also independent reviews have an important job in this respect. They do serve to record, to analyse and generalize, to an extent that communities and governments are unable to. Agencies don't have the time. They're too busy putting out bushfires.

Inductive learning from case studies of collaboration in environmental management

What approach should researchers follow in pursuing this role? Treating initiatives in collaborative environmental management as subjects for case studies would appear to offer a sound basis for such an approach. Support for such an approach in Australia has come from Mobbs and Dovers (1999, p131), who argued that a priority for the social sciences in respect of collaborative natural resource management is to 'isolate elements, strategies or mechanisms within particular experiences with potential for more generic application', and Dovers (1999b, p10), who commented that:

> Most cases can yield useable lessons both positive and negative, and the challenge is to build up a stock of these from across our collective experience, and apply these in various combinations to answer our future needs.

Comparative analysis of multiple case studies, as proposed here, is an established strategy for strengthening the external validity of individual case studies through data triangulation. The external validity of patterns in system behaviour and associated theoretical propositions identified in any case study is assessed ultimately by whether or not they are corroborated by other case studies, such that 'similar cases... help to show whether your theory can be generalised and dissimilar cases will help to extend or modify any theory' (Hussey and Hussey, 1997, p67).

The efficiency of data triangulation in strengthening external validity tends to be greatest when it comes from a single programme the research design of which comprises multiple cases (Yin, 1984). Data triangulation can also occur in the less structured way proposed above by Dovers, by utilizing the stock of relevant case studies from different projects as it accumulates over time. Indeed, this second strategy is the one that has been used chiefly by common property scholars in demonstrating that common property regimes are sometimes capable of managing common pool resources in an enduring way and in identifying design principles that can be used to help predict when such regimes will succeed or fail. The problem with this less structured strategy generally, and often also within past common property scholarship, is that it normally lacks the consistent conceptual basis and standardized approach to measuring particular variables that are required to facilitate comparability across case studies. Hence, Poteete and Ostrom (2003, p3) identified the following as one of two major obstacles normally encountered by common property scholars in learning about community-based natural resource management from multiple case studies:

> [T]he key factors expected to affect collective action and the outcomes of collective action are inconsistently conceptualized and measured... [C]ase study authors tend to identify different variables to study and making the findings from case studies comparable is extremely difficult. Contributions of empirical

research to the study of collective action will be limited unless the challenges of conceptual consistency and comparable data can be overcome.

Agrawal (2002, p41) argued that this obstacle has contributed significantly to a situation where each case study of successful community-based resource governance 'has generated different conclusions about what counts in 'successful' resource management'. The problem of comparability across case studies is made particularly formidable in the field of environmental and natural resource management because this field is truly cross disciplinary, with case studies undertaken variously by ecologists, biologists, anthropologists, political scientists, economists and sociologists (Edwards and Steins, 1998). Each discipline tends to use distinct methodological approaches and thus to focus on different questions, variables, relationships and units of analysis (e.g. individuals vs. groups). Despite the complications it entails for comparability across studies, cross-disciplinarity is indispensable in this field given that '[e]ach discipline and approach has something important to offer, and none (thus far) covers all aspects equally well' (Meinzen-Dick et al, 2004, p12).

The Institutional Analysis and Development framework

As mentioned above, the ideal means of achieving the comparability needed for data triangulation across multiple case studies involves research programmes wherein the design and analysis of different studies follows a common conceptual basis and a standardized approach to measuring particular variables. It would seem at least that the foundations of a common conceptual basis that can be used in such programmes are already in place, courtesy of the Institutional Analysis and Development (IAD) framework. This framework was developed at the Workshop in Political Theory and Policy Analysis, Indiana University, to facilitate cross-disciplinary research into complex institutions and governance structures. It is a framework, as distinct from a theory, since it:

> provides a metatheoretical language for thinking about diverse theories and their potential usefulness in addressing important questions of relevance to the analyst. At the conceptual level of a framework, theorists identify the broad working parts and their posited relationships that are used in an entire approach to a set of questions (Ostrom et al, 1994b, p23).

The IAD framework facilitates cross-disciplinary research by providing a language that is broader than the theoretical language of any particular discipline. In contrast to many so-called frameworks that are in fact tied closely to a single social science discipline, the IAD framework views all human decision situations (e.g. whether within markets, hierarchies or community arenas) as made up of the same set of elements or 'working parts'. It is well suited to thinking about alternative rational choice theories of collective action in so far as it 'starts from the individual as a basic unit of analysis to explain and predict individual behavior and resulting aggregated outcomes' and is primarily concerned with 'patterns of human action and the results that occur in interdependent choice-making situations' (Kiser and Ostrom, 1982, p181). It offers thereby a framework for institutional design, 'enabling us to analyse how rules interact with the physical and biological world, and culture, to condition the behavior of individuals, and produce social and environmental outcomes' (Ostrom, 1998b, p84).

This framework has been used by scholars at and associated with the Workshop for Political Theory and Policy Analysis to structure three major databases for the study of collective action in managing common pool resources. The first of these drew on existing case studies – mostly concerned with fisheries, groundwater basins and irrigation systems – and was used by Ostrom (1990) in elucidating her eight design principles that characterize robust self-organized regimes fostering sustainable resource use. The second of these databases is known as the Nepal Institutions and Irrigation Systems database. It contains data from more than 175 irrigation systems in Nepal, mostly obtained by coding existing case studies. The third database is subject to ongoing development within the International Forestry Resources and Institutions (IFRI) research programme. This programme commenced in 1993 and aims to provide a better understanding of how institutions affect incentives faced by forest users. Unlike the two earlier databases, the IFRI database relies primarily on fresh fieldwork rather than existing case studies. The programme involves a network of 13 collaborating research centres in 12 countries from Africa, Asia, Latin America, and North America. By early 2002, data for 173 sites with 264 forests and 302 forest user groups had been recorded in the programme's common database (Poteete and Ostrom, 2003).

The IAD framework has five 'working parts': (a) the decision maker; (b) the community affected by interdependent decision making; (c) events (or goods and services) that interacting individuals seek to provide and appropriate; (d) institutional arrangements guiding individual decisions; and (e) the decision situation in which individuals make choices (Kiser and Ostrom, 1982, p182). Analysts are free to select appropriate assumptions about the attributes of each working part. The relationship within this framework among the five working parts, actions, and outcomes is shown in Figure 7.1.

As Ostrom (1998a, p73) has observed, 'classification is a necessary step to develop a science'. Indeed, considerable progress has been made in developing classification systems for each of the working parts of the IAD framework. The classification system for institutional arrangements, for instance, begins by recognizing that the institutions, or rules, affecting the decision situations faced by individuals come from various sources, including: government legislation and regulation; policy decisions by private firms and voluntary associations; and norms, customs and other informal arrangements.

In addition, seven classes of rules have been distinguished. Rules in all classes interact to affect the structure of the decision situation. The seven classes are (Ostrom, 1999):

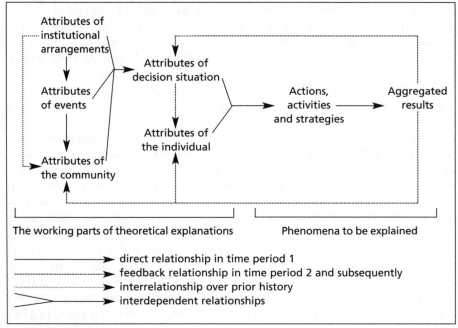

Source: Kiser and Ostrom (1982, Figure 7.1)

Figure 7.1 *The Institutional Analysis and Design framework*

- Position rules specify a set of positions (e.g. member of association, officer of association) and how many participants are to hold each position
- Boundary rules specify how participants enter or leave these positions (e.g. the criteria an individual must satisfy to gain membership of an association)
- Authority rules specify which set of actions is assigned to which position for a particular type of decision (e.g. how the board of an association should act if a member breaks a particular one of its rules)
- Aggregation rules specify the level of control that a participant in a position exercises in a particular decision (e.g. how the votes of different individual members regarding a decision are weighted and added)
- Scope rules specify the outcomes that are allowed, mandated or forbidden (e.g. a rule that restricts harvesting a certain fish species to a particular season)
- Information rules specify the access of each position to particular information for a particular type of decision (e.g. rules that give association members access to the evidence against them if they are charged with breaking an association rule)
- Payoff rules specify the benefits and costs assigned to particular combinations of actions and outcomes, thereby creating incentives (e.g. rules that prescribe the cost of becoming a member of an association, or that specify the privileges available to officers of the association).

Rules within each class can of course be distinguished further. In the case of boundary rules, for instance, 27 variables have been identified as being used in at least one common pool resource situation somewhere in the world. These variables are shown in Table 7.1. In many cases two or three of these variables are used in combination in defining a boundary rule. Particular rules of this kind can therefore be systematically codified according to the combination of variables used in their specification. Indeed, structured coding forms have been developed to help distinguish the types of rules affecting the behaviour of resource users in the field (as well as to distinguish more broadly the kinds of decision situations faced in the field) (Ostrom, 1999).

Table 7.1 *Variables used in specifying boundary rules for common pool resources*

Residency or membership	Personal characteristics	Relationship with resource
National	Ascribed	Continued use of resource
Regional	Age	
Local community	Caste	Long-term rights based on:
Organization (e.g. co-op)	Clan	Ownership of a proportion of
	Class	annual flow of resource units
	Ethnicity	Ownership of land
	Gender	Ownership of non-land asset
	Race	(e.g. fishing vessel berth)
	Acquired	Ownership of shares in a private
	Education level	organisation
	Skill test	Ownership of a share of the
		resource system
		Temporary use-rights acquired
		through:
		Auction
		Per-use fee
		Licenses
		Lottery
		Registration
		Seasonal fees
		Use of specified technology

Source: Ostrom (1999, Table 1)

Ostrom (1998b) has provided an overview of the variables upon which the classifications for the other working parts are based. For instance, the decision maker (or actor) is specified by four clusters of variables: the resources that the actor brings to the situation; the actor's valuations of states of the world and of actions; the actor's knowledge and information, and capabilities for acquiring, processing, retaining and using knowledge and information; and the actor's method of action selection. Variables by which community attributes are classified include: social norms; the level and nature of common understanding shared by potential participants; the extent to which people living in the community have homogeneous preferences; and the distribution of resources. As a final example, the attributes by which events (or goods) are distinguished include their rivalry, excludability and measurability.

The IAD framework recognizes that decision situations are linked across multiple levels of analysis, given that 'all rules are nested in another set of rules that define how the first set of rules can be changed' (Ostrom, 1990, p51). It has been found useful for the purposes of the IAD framework to distinguish three levels of rules: operational rules ('shallowest' level), collective choice rules and constitutional choice rules ('deepest' level). Operational rules relate to day-to-day decisions. Operational rules for an irrigation system, for example, may restrict the crops to be irrigated, the irrigation technologies that can be applied, or the volume of water than can be diverted from a supply channel. Collective choice rules govern how operational rules can be changed, and who can change them. An example of a collective choice rule for an irrigation system is a rule that requires a majority vote from irrigators using the system to allow use of a new technology. Constitutional choice rules are the rules to be followed in changing collective choice rules. A constitutional choice rule may, for example, require unanimous agreement among the irrigators using the system before any of the system's collective choice rules can be changed (Ostrom, 1998b).

When analysing the effects of a particular set of rules at a given level, the rules at 'deeper' levels must generally be held fixed for the purposes of tractability. This does not mean they should be ignored. The behavioural effects of the set of rules specifically being analysed can depend crucially on the rules in place at deeper levels. Where deeper-level rules provide for local user participation in changing the rules at the level of analysis being focused on, for instance, the proportion of local users regarding these latter rules as legitimate enough to warrant compliance may be markedly higher than would otherwise be the case. Analysing the effects of rules at a given level without accounting for the effects of existing deeper-level rules may therefore reduce considerably the explanatory power of the analysis. The IAD framework has made an important contribution to institutional analysis, therefore, in so far as it prompts researchers to account for a wider set of rules influencing behaviour at a particular level of analysis.

Institutional analysts seeking to learn from multiple case studies of institutional arrangements in order to inform the design of future arrangements need to compare the outcomes of those cases. The IAD framework does not prescribe any single criterion, or set of criteria, for such comparisons. It recognizes that a wide variety of such criteria exist – including Pareto efficiency, equity, accountability, adaptability, and conformance to social norms (e.g. in respect of promise-keeping) – and indeed that real-world institutional choices normally involve trade-offs between a number of criteria (Ostrom, 1998b).

Lessons learnt in developing institutional theory from case studies

As mentioned above, inductive learning from multiple case studies of collaborative community-based environmental management has been hampered in the past by a lack of cross-study comparability arising from the use of different conceptual approaches and inconsistent methods of measuring common variables. It seems that the database accumulating within the IFRI programme represents the greatest advance to date in addressing these obstacles. Unlike its two predecessors, the IFRI database has relied primarily on new case studies rather than existing ones. This has provided the opportunity to achieve increased consistency of concepts and measurement methods across cases by developing a common set of data collection instruments and also common methods for collecting data. The collaborating research centres undertaking the data collection consist of scholars committed to using these IFRI protocols for data collection and submitting their data to the central IFRI database (Poteete and Ostrom, 2003).

A further potential advantage of the IFRI database over its predecessors derives from the large number of cases it covers as a result of being able to draw on an international network of research centres. The importance of this potential advantage has been highlighted by Agrawal's (2002, p46) observation that '[p]roblems of incomplete model specification and omitted variables in hypothesis testing are widespread in the literature on common property'. This state of affairs has arisen, he explained, because 'even the best known studies of the commons usually have no more than 15 to 30 cases in their sample' (ibid, p71). If data triangulation is to provide a rigorous check on the external validity of patterns observed across multiple case studies in how particular explanatory variables affect a dependent variable, then the sample of cases generating data on all those variables must be: (a) greater than the number of explanatory variables under investigation; and (b) carefully chosen to control for other, including contextual, variables expected to affect the dependent variable. These conditions are not trivial for research explaining the performance of community-based management of common pool resources, given that Agrawal (ibid, p65) has concluded – from a comprehensive survey of leading research in this area – that at least 30 theoretically important variables help to explain such performance, there are important interactions between some of these variables, and '[t]he set of variables that constitutes the context is potentially infinite'.

With comparable data from a large number of case studies available to them, researchers within the IFRI research network are better positioned to surmount the problems of incomplete model specification and missing variables that previous researchers in this area have run into (Poteete and Ostrom, 2003). Nevertheless, a research strategy as ambitious as this 'is an enormously expensive affair in terms of time, finances, and keeping one's involvement in the case at bay' (Agrawal, 2002, p71). Moreover, some significant problems with data comparability remain in the IFRI research programme due to difficulties in controlling for all key contextual differences, particularly across biophysical, cultural and political zones. Where cross-national analyses have occurred within the programme, a lack of universality across national boundaries in some key relationships of analytical interest has sometimes been revealed. Hence, the number of cross-national analyses within the programme has remained limited (Poteete and Ostrom, 2003). The scope to design the programme to control for contextual differences has been constrained in part because 'case selection can sometimes depend on availability of funding, an individual researcher's interests, and the ease of establishing collaborative partnerships with research institutions in different countries' (Agrawal, 2002, p76).

These continuing limitations on comparative analysis across the large international set of cases documented in the IFRI programme, despite the large investments in it, point to the advantages of achieving the data triangulation required through a number of steps. Agrawal (ibid) has proposed, along these lines, a two-step approach to institutional analysis through multiple case studies which emphasizes not only careful research design but also careful case selection. The first step involves studies focused on improving our understanding of specific causal relationships indicated by existing theory, in order to narrow the range of relationships and variables to be investigated in the second step. Although the first step involves comparison of multiple case studies, its focus on relationships involving subsets of the full set of variables deemed relevant by existing theory means that the number of cases required for data triangulation can be kept relatively small. The purpose of the second step is to comprehensively investigate the full range of causal relationships supported empirically in the first step as helping to explain the performance of institutional arrangements in managing common pool resources. Since this step involves analysis of how all these relationships work together to help explain institutional performance, and consequently accounts for a large set of variables, it cannot proceed rigorously without a large number of case studies containing comparable data on each of these variables. Nevertheless, the number of case studies required for the second step will be less than would be the case without the first step preceding it, provided the first step has successfully narrowed down the range of variables to be accounted for. This number can be reduced further by using prior knowledge to ensure that the sample of cases selected for comparison exhibits substantial variation in respect of the variables of theoretical interest and minimal variation in respect of other, including contextual, variables. Poteete and Ostrom (2003, p22) identified accordingly the advantages in the IFRI programme from adopting 'a strategy of testing hypotheses first with data from a single country, and then scaling up to cross-national analyses'.

The proposed strategy

The focus of Agrawal's (2002) two-step approach to theoretical development through comparative analysis of multiple case studies is on research into common property management of common pool resources. Nevertheless, it is relevant also for research into collaborative management of such resources – involving as it does cooperation between common property and state property regimes – given that the number of variables affecting such management is certainly no less than the number affecting common property management. Hence, it is proposed here that this approach be used as a basis for research seeking to explain the performance of collaborative environmental management, including research by economists.

The importance in multi-case analysis of collaborative environmental management of ensuring cross-case comparability of data has been emphasized recently by Conley and Moote (2003). The strategy envisaged here for addressing this challenge would follow the lead of the IFRI research programme in using a common set of data collection instruments for all case studies included in a programme, as well as common methods for collecting data. The data collection instruments would be consistent with the IAD framework and build wherever possible on the classification and codification systems already developed for defining variables consonant with that framework. The IFRI database and data collection instruments built in like manner on those created in compiling the Nepal Institutions and Irrigation Systems database, after the Forest, Trees and People Program of the FAO encouraged development of a similar database for the forestry sector.

Given the problems of cross-case comparability encountered in the IFRI programme as a result of selecting cases from diverse biophysical, cultural and political contexts, it seems prudent in any research programme focused on collaborative environmental management to begin by selecting cases for comparison that differ as little as possible contextually – at least until the influence of theoretically important variables on institutional performance within a given type of context is understood well enough that the research focus can shift to investigating the influence of contextual variables. In many countries nowadays, and indeed in many regions within them, there are enough cases of collaborative environmental management underway within particular sectors (e.g. forestry, fisheries, irrigation, biodiversity, watershed management) that it is not necessary to search for additional cases from other countries or regions to obtain enough cases for rigorous comparison. The external validity of patterns found across cases sharing a similar context can subsequently be explored by checking whether those patterns also exist within other, contextually different, sets of cases. Where we discover in this process that the effects of some theoretically important variables on the performance of collaborative institutional arrangements are context sensitive, it will be essential then to devise research designs capable of identifying how particular contextual variables interact with particular theoretical variables to influence the performance of such arrangements. It is envisaged that such research designs would be informed by the framework for analysis of institutional performance in common pool resource management presented by Edwards and Steins (1998). This framework elaborates an earlier framework developed by Oakerson (1986; 1992), which is a version of the IAD framework specifically concerned with institutional arrangements for managing common pool resources. The elaboration of the Oakerson framework included incorporation of 'contextual factors' as a new working part.

A particular challenge in such a research effort involves comparing the performance of the different institutional arrangements for collaborative environmental management studied. A wide range of criteria for evaluating the performance of such programmes have been proposed. As Conley and Moote

(2003, p375) observed, '[t]he deeper one delves, the more criteria one can identify, for each of the oft-cited benefits and criticisms of collaboration can easily be turned into criteria for evaluating specific collaborative efforts'. From several lists of evaluative criteria proposed for collaborative environmental management in North America, they synthesized the list of 'typical' evaluation criteria reproduced in Table 7.2.

Table 7.2 *Typical evaluation criteria for collaborative environmental management*

Process criteria	Broadly shared vision
	Clear, feasible goals
	Diverse, inclusive participation
	Participation by local government
	Linkages to individual groups beyond primary participants
	Open, accessible and transparent process
	Clear, written plan
	Consensus-based decision making
	Decisions regarded as just
	Consistent with existing laws and policies
Environmental outcome criteria	Improved habitat
	Land protected from development
	Improved water quality
	Changed land management practices
	Biological diversity preserved
	Soil and water resources conserved
Socioeconomic outcome criteria	Relationships built or strengthened
	Increased trust
	Participants' gained knowledge and understanding
	Increased employment
	Improved capacity for dispute resolution
	Changes in existing institutions or creation of new institutions

Source: Conley and Moote (2003, Table 1)

Refining the strategy for economic research

The stance taken in this book, reflected in the political economic approach to analysing the cost effectiveness of institutional options proposed in Chapter 4, is that the criteria used in comparing the performance of different institutional arrangements for collaborative environmental management should accord with the values, preference rankings or goals of the political community on whose behalf the evaluation is being undertaken. This book is concerned primarily with the economics of pursuing successful collaborative environmental management through adaptive management. The economics focus presumes that an important goal in this pursuit is efficiency, given the textbook definition of the economic problem as that of allocating scarce means among competing ends. Nevertheless, as explained in Chapter 4, the Paretian criterion used in mainstream economics to compare the efficiency of institutional options derives from a mechanistic worldview that differs markedly from the complexity-based worldview responsible in recent years for the strengthening consensus that adaptive management is the appropriate approach to determining which option is likely to perform best in a specific context. An approach to measuring economic efficiency that is consistent with the worldview underlying advocacy for adaptive management was therefore proposed in that chapter.

The political economy approach proposed in this book for comparing the economic efficiency of institutional options focuses on identifying the option that minimizes the aggregate cost across all relevant actors of achieving one or more policy objectives (e.g. revegetation targets for reversing biodiversity decline) agreed, at least for the time being, within the relevant political community. This approach differs from the Paretian cost effectiveness measure of economic efficiency in two important ways. First, the effects of path dependencies and associated instances of 'lock-in' on the transformation and transaction costs incurred by individual actors are accounted for rather than assumed small enough to safely ignore. Second, the value judgements underlying the aggregation of costs incurred by individual actors are decided ultimately by the relevant political community rather than imposed 'objectively' by the analyst.

The first of these departures from the mainstream measure of economic efficiency means that precise predictions of the efficiency consequences of alternative institutional options can no longer be justified theoretically. Accounting for path dependencies introduces two categories of costs that are neglected when institutional options are evaluated using the mainstream measure of cost effectiveness. In Chapter 4, these two types of costs were called 'institutional lock-in costs' and 'technological lock-in costs'. These costs arise because:

- institutional choices are typically complex due to the path dependencies they unleash;
- humans faced with complex choices can only be boundedly rational, so are unlikely to make any such choices optimally at the outset;
- any choice made at the outset leads to path dependencies that increase the resources needed to reverse that choice when, in all likelihood, new information arises revealing it to have been suboptimal.

In principle at least, the costs in the other four categories that were distinguished – static transaction costs, institutional transition costs, static transformation costs and technological transition costs – can be predicted precisely and appropriately through the method of comparative statics. Although substantial challenges remain in predicting static transaction costs and institutional transition costs using comparative statics, there are grounds for optimism that these can be overcome with innovation in analytical and data collection techniques. As explained in Chapter 4, however, comparative static derivation of precise predictions for institutional lock-in costs and technological lock-in costs is inappropriate methodologically. This is because the method of comparative statics neglects the increasing returns responsible for the path dependencies that generate these costs. Hence, it precisely predicts unique equilibrium values for these costs when the actual values have multiple possible equilibria or else are in continuing non-equilibrium. Without precise predictions for the costs in these two categories that can be defended theoretically, clearly it is not defensible to generate for any institutional option a precise prediction for the aggregate costs to be incurred across all six categories.

Since it lacks a capacity to precisely predict the efficiency repercussions of institutional choices, the political economy approach to institutional analysis proposed here fails to satisfy the standard set in mainstream economics for ex ante institutional analysis. This capacity could be restored without serious loss of analytical accuracy if it were reasonable to assume that the sum of institutional and technological lock-in costs is normally insignificant compared with the sum of costs associated with the other cost categories, or at least that the sum of institutional and technological lock-in costs generally varies little across institutional options. However, such assumptions do not reasonably reflect the reality of most institutional choices, especially choices concerned with the problems of institutional choice prone to path dependency that we typically face in trying to shift towards a sustainable path of development through collaborative environmental management. To adopt these assumptions would therefore be to risk, particularly for the kinds of problems we are concerned with here, non-trivial losses of accuracy in predicting optimal institutional choices.

Before proceeding to consider how institutional and technological lock-in costs might be predicted for ex ante institutional analysis, let us first consider how the political economy criterion for evaluating cost effectiveness in institutional choice proposed in this book might be applied within an ex post multi-case analysis of experiences in collaborative environmental management based on the IAD framework. The key differences from a Paretian cost effectiveness analysis are threefold. First, data would be collected from each case in respect of the costs incurred in all of the six cost categories represented in the criterion (a comprehensive Paretian analysis would neglect to collect data for two of these categories). Second, the cost data in respect of all six categories would be accounted for when calculating the aggregate cost incurred in each case. Third, the cost data would be collected and processed in a form that permits calculation of the aggregate cost incurred in each case in accordance with a social welfare function provided ultimately by the relevant political community. Where the social welfare function is influenced by the polluter pays principle and weights the costs incurred by polluters as a result of institutional options less heavily than the costs incurred by those subject to the pollution, for instance, then cost data would be collected in a way that allows separate calculation of the costs incurred by polluters and pollutees. As in Paretian cost effectiveness analysis, data on the progress made in all cases against policy objectives (e.g. hectares of land revegetated with prescribed species) would be collected so that cost effectiveness could be calculated in each case by dividing this measure of progress by the aggregate costs (weighted aggregate costs in the case of the political economy approach) incurred in achieving this progress.

The task of collecting data on costs incurred in all six categories will rarely be easy, but it will be easier in the kind of ex post analysis with which we are presently concerned – where we are measuring what has occurred already – than in an ex ante analysis – where we must predict what will occur. Even so, it may not always be possible or affordable to estimate in monetary terms the costs already incurred within some of the cost categories, especially for the categories associated with transaction costs. Where this is an issue for a particular cost category, there will often be enough information available to the analyst – if she or he consults with those involved across the different cases – to quantitatively compare the costs incurred across cases in that category using an ordinal scale (e.g. a five-step scale bounded by 'very high costs incurred' at one end and 'very low costs incurred' at the other). This would leave us with costs in some categories measured monetarily and costs in some other categories measured using an ordinal scale. The challenge would then be to combine the monetary and non-monetary measures for each case into a single cost measure that could be used to calculate its cost effectiveness. The best way to address this challenge would seem to be through assisting the relevant political community to choose an algorithm to be applied across all cases in converting the different cost measures into a 'common currency' so that they can be aggregated. There has been considerable experience with developing algorithms of this kind in multi-criteria analysis (e.g., Hajkowicz et al, 2000) that could be drawn upon usefully in pursuing this strategy.

A further challenge with using the political economy approach for ex post cost effectiveness analysis of collaborative institutional arrangements is that costs in two of the cost categories represented in that approach – institutional lock-in costs and technological lock-in costs – will usually not have been incurred fully by the time the analysis takes place. Since such costs arise from path dependencies, they may in fact continue indefinitely. Ultimately, therefore, a capacity to predict institutional lock-in costs and technological lock-in costs needs to be developed if the political economy approach is to be applied comprehensively either for ex post or ex ante analysis of collaborative institutional arrangements.

The appropriate way forward in developing such capacity would seem to be through a multi-case research programme structured along the lines proposed in the previous section. The case studies comprising such a programme would need to be of long enough duration (probably no shorter than a decade) to allow at least the early consequences of the institutional choices made for path dependency, and thus for institutional lock-in costs and technological lock-in costs, to become apparent. In addition to collecting data for measuring these costs over the life of the project, the programme would also focus on collecting data on variables that the existing theoretical and empirical literature suggests contribute to institutional path dependency and thus, by implication, to the magnitude of these costs. For instance, Challen (2000) has hypothesized that institutional path dependency, and thus institutional lock-in costs, will be greater the more that property rights are decentralized to lower levels of an institutional hierarchy.

The cases would be chosen for their diversity in respect of these variables, and for their relative uniformity in respect of other, including contextual, variables. The programme would seek to establish whether the variables suggested by the existing literature to affect institutional path dependency do have such an effect and, if so, to determine how these variables interact in establishing the path dependency that we observe. It would seek also to identify inductively any other behavioural regularities across cases that might serve as hypotheses to be tested in subsequent research programmes focused on further developing a theory explaining path dependency of institutional arrangements for collaborative environmental management. Such theory would be of practical use in helping us predict the institutional lock-in costs and technological lock-in costs arising from particular institutional options, including for ex ante analyses of institutional choices. These predictions will necessarily be rough (probably expressed in ordinal units more often than in monetary amounts), and also heavily qualified given the strong influence that random events (e.g. emergence of leaders, results of national elections) can exert on institutional path dependency. However, that is the inescapable nature of the complexity we face in analysing institutional choices.

Once predictions are generated from such a programme for the institutional lock-in costs and technological lock-in costs of a particular institutional option in a particular context, they can be used to help estimate these costs for ex post cost effectiveness analysis of institutional options in accordance with the approach proposed in this book. As information from ex post analyses of this kind accumulates in a database structured in accordance with the IAD framework, the capacity to identify patterns in the cost effectiveness of particular kinds of institutional options in particular contexts will expand – permitting the cost effectiveness of particular options to be predicted for ex ante analyses with increasing confidence – albeit always recognizing that the predictions we can hope to make will at best be rough and highly contingent on how random events unfold. The capacity of economic analysis to help translate the concept of adaptive management successfully into practice will grow accordingly.

Countering scepticism with knowledge

Despite the frustrations experienced internationally in realizing the collaborative vision for environmental management, the blame for lack of progress seems to lie not with the vision but with the ad hoc, business-pretty-much-as-usual approach typically followed in its pursuit. Politicians and government officers often have valid reasons for treading cautiously in pursuing the collaborative vision. It is understandable that they are half-hearted in decentralizing management tasks to community and other lower-level actors until they have established trust that institutional arrangements for collaborative environmental management can be designed and implemented that enable those tasks to be performed more successfully than is already the case. Where Progressive beliefs to the effect that the interests of communities and other civil groups are inevitably at odds with the interests of the broader public remain embedded in their mental models and reflected in the dominant theories of collective action, formidable obstacles lie ahead in establishing this trust. Strong leadership from within government is clearly vital here, but another powerful way of turning around these beliefs is by accumulating evidence demonstrating them to be mistaken. It is contended that the strategy outlined above for social scientists, including economists, to follow in accumulating such evidence, and in increasing the confidence with which the performance of particular collaborative institutional arrangements in specific contexts can be predicted, offers longer-term promise in this direction.

8

Myth, Enlightenment and Economics

An economics capable of comprehending the collaborative vision for environmental management and analysing credibly the institutional choices arising in its pursuit has been presented above. This economics recognizes that the vision – one wherein collaboration between different stakeholders in making institutional choices leads them to cooperate with one another more voluntarily in implementing the chosen options than they would otherwise – can only be appreciated in social settings of any significant scale if the dynamics of the social-ecological systems faced with these choices are modelled as involving increasing returns (positive feedbacks) as well as diminishing returns (negative feedbacks). This is because the emergence and growth of voluntary cooperation within large groups occurs through the increasing returns involved in mutually reinforcing relationships between reciprocity, trust and voluntary cooperation.

Nevertheless, increasing returns constitute a two-edged sword. Given favourable circumstances, they can indeed lead to voluntary cooperation escalating in a virtuous circle with reciprocity and trust. In less favourable circumstances, however, they can 'lock-in' low levels of voluntary cooperation, or else lead existing levels of voluntary cooperation to unravel in a vicious circle with reciprocity and trust. It becomes clear, therefore, that the ability of collaborative systems of environmental management to increase voluntary implementation of the kinds of institutional options required for effective pursuit of sustainable development, and thus reduce the costs (including social and political) of this pursuit to levels low enough for political obstacles to this pursuit to become surmountable, depends on how effectively such systems can create and maintain circumstances conducive to the emergence, growth and sustenance of the kinds of virtuous circles referred to above.

To be sure, collaborative organizational systems offer significant potential for establishing and fuelling virtuous circles of this kind. One way in which they do so is by breaking social groups too large and impersonal for the emergence of voluntary cooperation into multiple smaller groups working in partnership, thereby providing increased opportunities for trust, reciprocity and voluntary cooperation to emerge and build on one another. Another way is by offering increased scope for deliberative communication among stakeholders. Such communication can allow the mental models and perceived interests of stakeholders to converge somewhat as they learn more about their interdependencies, and thereby increase the likelihood of stakeholders agreeing on solutions to their shared problems to which they feel committed – and thus the likelihood of individual stakeholders being prepared to try voluntary cooperation on the basis of reciprocity.

Realizing this potential, however, is no simple matter. A system shaped significantly by increasing returns is known as a complex adaptive system. The consequences of consciously intervening in such a system are typically sensitive to fine details of the intervention as well as to random events the importance of which often becomes apparent only in retrospect. Even where a collaborative system of environmental management is designed and implemented at the outset with the best of intentions and available knowledge, therefore, a significant chance remains, given human cognitive limitations, that the system in its original form will not succeed in gaining significant voluntary cooperation with its management decisions. Certainly, it is improbable that the system established at the outset will be the optimal one for promoting voluntary cooperation given actual circumstances at the outset. Even if it were, it would not remain optimal once those circumstances changed.

This portrayal of the challenge of realizing the collaborative vision for environmental management echoes a key lesson that Huxham and Vangen (2000b) drew from a decade of research into collaborative partnerships working within various policy domains in the UK including health promotion, environmental conservation, and economic and social regeneration. The lesson was this:

> [I]f you are seriously concerned to achieve success in [collaborative] partnership, be prepared to nurture... and nurture... and nurture. All of the activities associated with partnership require sensitivity and attention to detail... and because of the dynamics, this can never be relaxed (Huxham and Vangen, 2000b, p307).

This lesson was heeded in developing the approach proposed in this book for the economic analysis of institutional choices arising in pursuit of the collaborative vision. This approach recognizes that optimality in complex institutional choices can at best be identified and tracked only approximately through a continual process of adaptive management; that is, a process in which the institutional options chosen at any juncture are treated systematically as experiments generating knowledge of value for subsequently adapting those options. It recognizes also that opportunities within complex social-ecological systems to nurture or adapt institutional choices as knowledge accumulates can be constrained considerably as a result of the path dependencies that increasing returns tend to create. Consider an institutional choice made centrally, for instance, that assigns the responsibility for performing a certain management task to a government agency in ignorance of the fact that a local community was already undertaking that task successfully on the basis of its social capital (i.e. social norms, trust and interpersonal networks). Even if those responsible for the choice came eventually to realize their mistake, reversing it may no longer be feasible given the speed with which social capital accumulated over generations can unravel when its role is supplanted, and because the agency staff employed on the task may oppose its return to the community. The approach to economic analysis of complex institutional choices proposed in this book accounts for such constraints on future institutional choices arising from current institutional choices in terms of their effect in increasing the total costs (transformation costs plus transaction costs) of ongoing adaptation towards optimal institutional choices. Importantly, given our focus on choices concerned with realizing the collaborative vision, this approach can account for differences between current institutional options (e.g. in respect of their fit with existing local norms) on how they affect ongoing trust, social capital more generally, and voluntary cooperation.

The economics of collaborative systems of environmental management proposed here analyses such systems, as well as the wider social-ecological systems they seek to influence, as the complex adaptive systems that they are. This approach differs from the mainstream economic approach to analysing institutional choices – that associated with the dominant strand of the new institutional economics – which continues to analyse the systems subject to such choices as mechanistic systems (i.e. through the method of comparative statics). This commitment harks in part from a sincere and deeply-rooted belief among many mainstream economists, following from how science has been understood publicly given the modernist beliefs associated with the Progressive vision, that economics cannot claim to be a science unless it retains the predictive precision that mechanistic analysis can deliver – at least if various simplifying assumptions, including that increasing returns can be safely ignored, are accepted. It also follows less nobly from economists seeking to capitalize on the continuing widespread Progressive view among politicians and public administrators that policy advice is useful to the extent that it is precise and therefore unambiguous. More than a few economists are reluctant to admit publicly that analytical tools derived from comparative statics are ill-suited for complex policy problems because to do so 'would have unhappy implications for the agreeable prospects of attracting consulting contracts and grants from executive branch agencies' (Bromley, 2004, p78).

It may be unrealistic to expect, therefore, a rush among mainstream economists, including environmental and resource economists, to embrace the political economy approach to cost effectiveness analysis of institutional choices proposed here. Nevertheless, momentum is building within economics more generally towards acknowledging the limits of comparative statics in analysing complex policy problems with reasonable accuracy. This momentum has been demonstrated most obviously by recently growing interest in the complexity approach to economics which emerged from concerns that 'economics has found a simple structure, but only at the cost of assumptions that make the theory difficult, if not impossible, to relate to empirical reality' (Colander, 2000b, p33). Bromley (2004, p88) referred to related tensions in respect of the narrower field of environmental economics as follows:

> Some of us may take great comfort in the thought that 300–500 environmental economists remain committed to prescriptive consequentialism [i.e. the rationale for the Paretian comparative static approach to policy analysis] ... At the risk of putting too

fine a point on it, applied economists who still believe in consequentialism as the true guide to correct public policy are seen as out of touch with the recent advances in economic thinking – and they have been for at least two decades now.

Economists are far from alone in finding their efforts at coming to terms with the collaborative vision for environmental management in particular, and with the sustainability ethic underlying this vision, impeded by lock-in to inherited beliefs, values and institutions. As Beck (1992, p11) highlighted, public discourse in the industrialized world remains firmly under the spell of the 'myth of industrial society'. This myth asserts in essence that the cultural fundamentals of a thoroughly modern world are already settled, and implies accordingly that the development path we embarked upon armed with the modernist beliefs responsible for the scientific and industrial revolutions requires fine tuning at most. Sustainability discourse, on the other hand, implies that the welfare of future human generations is unlikely to be maintained at current levels without some deep cultural changes in terms of beliefs, values and institutions. Efforts until now to shift onto a sustainable path of development have been restricted in large part to fairly superficial institutional changes. Connor and Dovers (2004, p209) have observed, as follows, that the required deeper-level institutional changes will not be possible without complementary efforts to bring about publicly held values congruent with those changes:

> [S]uccessful institutional systems do not work through rigid and continuous enforcement of rules... They are effective because there exists a general consensus on the values represented in the rules – that the rules are fair and reasonable according to those values. Hence sustainability can only be viable when socially held values become aligned with those implicit in a sustainability ethic.

Changes in publicly held values of the requisite magnitude cannot be expected to occur overnight. Connor and Dovers (ibid, p208) suggested that 'perhaps six to ten decades is not an unreasonable expectation' for how long it will take to bring such changes about. For similar reasons, the reluctance of mainstream economics to engage credibly with the complexity of pursuing sustainability via collaborative environmental management can be expected to persist until its underlying beliefs and values cease to become incompatible with such engagement. Some indication of how long we could wait for this might be gleaned from one leading economist's speculation that by 2030 most economic researchers will accept that the economy is best analysed as a complex adaptive system (Colander, 2000a).

The foregoing highlights the importance of patience in pursuing the collaborative vision. Given the continuing prevalence of beliefs and values incongruent with this vision, including within mainstream economics, which retains considerable influence over contemporary policy formulation, it will often be unrealistic to expect collaborative institutional arrangements to demonstrate significant improvements in environmental management within even a decade. This patience has been in short supply to date, and pursuit of the collaborative vision has received much unfair criticism as a result. As the progenitor of adaptive management, C. S. Holling (2004, p8) has written, '[p]robably the greatest difficulty [in achieving a sustainable, adaptive system] is to communicate the issue of time'. It is a rare person, he observed, that can transcend short-term issues concerned with 'fast variables' and focus on the longer-term changes involving 'slow variables' needed to sustain an adaptive system. The fast variables in human societies tend to be the economic ones (e.g. financial return on investment), while the slow variables tend to be cultural and normative (e.g. ideologies, values, trust, norms, leadership capacities, quality of mass media, educational curricula, and so on). If we are serious about realizing the collaborative vision before it is too late, therefore, it is crucial that we begin to work on these kinds of slow variables without delay. A key slow variable in respect of economists arriving at beliefs and values congruent with the collaborative vision clearly relates to the curricula for teaching new generations of economists at high schools and universities. A further key slow variable, this time in respect of the wider public arriving at such beliefs and values, relates to access of new generations of citizens, politicians and public officials to an education which shares with them what has been learned about the factors contributing to success and failure in collaborative environmental management.

The sustainability ethic, together with its constituent collaborative vision for environmental management, cannot help but be deeply unsettling to those many people today, including mainstream economists, keeping faith with the myth of industrial society. These ideas have emerged from a sense that humans have entered a period of cultural transformation the like of which we have witnessed only twice previously: agricultural settlement by the first hunter-gatherers and the industrial revolution. To sit on our hands and avert our gaze from the slow variables keeping us locked into the myth of industrial society, and thus on a detour from the avowed modern quest of Enlightenment, is to increase the likelihood that our transition to a sustainable path of development will take the form of a 'crash landing' (Holling, 2004). To act decisively, on the other hand, will require some dearly held beliefs and values to be given up. As unsettling as this will be, it will also open up immense opportunities for human creativity. After all, '[w]hat the sustainable world will be like we can only guess. How we will get there, and learn to be content with it, are equally mysterious' (Connor and Dovers, 2004, p209). The cultural challenge ahead is for enough of us – within governments, corporations, communities, subdisciplines of economics and so on – to embrace these opportunities such that transition to a sustainable, collaborative path of development becomes feasible sooner and smoothly, rather than later and perhaps catastrophically. It is hoped that this book will help with part of this challenge by assisting economists to comprehend the collaborative vision for environmental management and envisage how their formidable talents can be applied usefully in analysing the complex institutional choices that will continue to arise in its pursuit.

Notes

Chapter 1 Progress, Sustainability and Economics

1 This section draws extensively from Norgaard (1994).

Chapter 3 Developments in Collective Action Theory for Commons Management

1 In the case of a symmetric externality, action by one agent affects another who *is* in a position to reciprocate. With an asymmetric externality, action by one party affects another who *is not* in a position to reciprocate (Stevenson, 1991).

Chapter 4 An Economics for Collaborative Environmental Management

1 The term social-ecological system refers to 'the subset of social systems in which some of the interdependent relationships among humans are mediated through interactions with biophysical and non-human biological units' (Anderies et al, 2004, p3).
2 Aside from 'static transaction costs' and 'dynamic transaction costs', the names given here and below to the different classes of transaction costs are revised from those used by Challen (2000).
3 It is important to recognize that some leading contributors to the NIE including Douglas North (1990, 2005) and Elinor Ostrom (1990, 2005) have not resorted to this strategy, and continue to emphasize the need to account for bounded rationality and path dependency when analysing complex institutional choices.

Chapter 6 From Antagonism to Trust: Collaborative Salinity Management in Australia's Murray Darling Basin

1 This refers to the Irrigation Management Board (IMB) for the region that the Government established under the Water Resources Act. Mr Martin commented that 'The Department [of Water Resources] was directed [by its Minister] to give the Board a major say in the running of the irrigation districts, because the Government wanted to move toward privatization'. Mr Baxter was Chairperson of the IMB by the time that deliberations over local implementation of the LWMPs had begun.

References

Agrawal, A. (2002) 'Common resources and institutional sustainability', in Ostrom, E., Dietz, T., Dolšak, N., Stern, P. C., Stonich, S. and Weber, E. U. (eds) *The Drama of the Commons*, National Academy Press, Washington, DC, pp41–85

Agrawal, A. and Gibson, C. C. (eds) (2001) *Communities and the Environment: Ethnicity, Gender, and the State in Community-based Conservation*, Rutgers University Press, New Brunswick

Alchian, A. A. (1950) 'Uncertainty, evolution and economic theory', *Journal of Political Economy*, vol 58, pp211–221

Allen, D. W. (1991) 'What are transaction costs?', *Research in Law and Economics*, vol 14, pp1–18

Altman, M. (2000) 'A behavioral model of path dependency: The economics of profitable inefficiency and market failure', *Journal of Socio-Economics*, vol 29, pp127–145

Anderies, J. M., Janssen, M. A. and Ostrom, E. (2004) 'A framework to analyze the robustness of social-ecological systems from an institutional perspective', *Ecology and Society*, vol 9, p18, www.ecologyandsociety.org/vol9/iss1/art18

Anderson, T. L. and Leal, D. R. (1991) *Free Market Environmentalism*, Pacific Research Institute for Public Policy, San Francisco

Andersson, K. (2003) 'What motivates municipal governments? Uncovering the institutional incentives for municipal governance of forest resources in Bolivia', *Journal of Environment and Development*, vol 12, pp5–27

Andersson, K. P., Gibson, C. C. and Lehoucq, F. (2004) 'The politics of decentralizing natural resource policy', *PSOnline*, July, pp1–7, www.apsanet.org

Annan, K. (2002a) 'Sustainability not a "pious invocation" but a "call to concrete action" Secretary-General tells European Forum for Sustainable Development', Press Release SG/SM/8150 ENV/DEV/626, United Nations, New York, www.un.org/News/Press/docs/2002/sgsm8150.doc.htm

Annan, K. (2002b) '"Towards a Sustainable Future": The American Museum of Natural History's Annual Environmental Lecture', United Nations, New York, http://sustsci.harvard.edu/keydocs/fulltext/annan_amnh_020514.pdf

Appleby, P. H. (1949) *Policy and Administration*, University of Alabama Press, Birmingham

Arrow, K. J. (1951) *Social Choice and Individual Values*, John Wiley and Sons, New York

Arrow, K. J. (1974) *The Limits of Organization*, Norton, New York

Arrow, K. J. (1987) 'Reflections on the essays', in Feiwel, G. (ed) *Arrow and the Foundations of the Theory of Economic Policy*, New York University Press, New York, pp727–734

Arrow, K. J. and Raynaud, H. (1986) *Social Choice and Multicriterion Decision-Making*, MIT Press, Cambridge, MA

Arthur, W. B. (1988) 'Self-reinforcing mechanisms in economics', in Anderson, P. W., Arrow, K. J. and Pines, D. (eds) *The Economy as a Complex Evolving System*, Addison Wesley, Redwood City, pp9–31

Arthur, W. B. (1989) 'Competing technologies, increasing returns, and lock-in by historical events', *Economic Journal*, vol 99, no 394, pp116–131

Arthur, W. B. (1994) 'Inductive reasoning and bounded rationality', *American Economic Review*, vol 84, pp406–411

Axelrod, R. (1984) *The Evolution of Cooperation*, Basic Books, New York

Bagadion, B. U. (1997) 'The National Irrigation Administration's participatory irrigation management program in the Philippines', in Krishna, A., Uphoff, N. and Esman, M. J. (eds) *Reasons for Hope: Instructive Experiences in Rural Development*, Kumarian Press, West Hartford, pp153–165

Baland, J.-M., and Platteau, J.-P. (1996) *Halting Degradation of Natural Resources: Is There a Role for Rural Communities?*, Clarendon Press, Oxford

Ball, T., and Dagger, R. (1995) *Political Ideologies and the Democratic Ideal*, 2nd edition, HarperCollins College Publishers, New York

Barbier, E. B. (1987) 'The concept of sustainable economic development', *Environmental Conservation*, vol 14, pp101–110

Barkow, J. H., Cosmides, L. and Tooby, J. (eds) (1992) *The Adapted Mind: Evolutionary Psychology and the Generation of Culture*, Oxford University Press, Oxford

Barnett, H., and Morse, C. (1963) *Scarcity and Growth: The Economics of Natural Resource Availability*, John Hopkins University Press, Baltimore

Batie, S. S. (1989) 'Sustainable development: Challenges to the profession of agricultural economics', *American Journal of Agricultural Economics*, vol 71, pp1083–1101

Beck, U. (1992) *Risk Society: Towards a New Modernity,* Sage Publications, London

Bellamy, J. A., and Johnson, A. K. L. (2000) 'Integrated resource management: Moving from rhetoric to practice in Australian agriculture', *Environmental Management*, vol 25, pp265–280

Berger, P. L., and Neuhaus, R. J. (1977) *To Empower People: The Role of Mediating Structures in Public Policy*, American Enterprise Institute, Washington, DC

Berger, P. L., and Neuhaus, R. J. (1996) 'Peter L. Berger and Richard John Neuhaus respond', in Novak, M. (ed) *To Empower People: From State to Civil Society*, AEI Press, Washington, DC, pp145–154

Berkes, F. (2002) 'Cross-scale institutional linkages: Perspectives from the bottom up', in Ostrom, E., Dietz, T., Dolšak, N., Stern, P. C., Stonich, S. and Weber, E. U. (eds) *The Drama of the Commons*, National Academy Press, Washington, DC, pp293–321

Berkes, F., Colding, J. and Folke, C. (eds) (2003) *Navigating Social-Ecological Systems: Building Resilience for Complexity and Change*, Cambridge University Press, New York

Betts, K. (1997) 'Social capital and cultural diversity', Paper presented to the Social Capital Conference, 11 July, Brisbane

Boulding, K. E. (1970) *Economics as a Science*, McGraw-Hill, New York

British Institute of International and Comparative Law (2003) 'Subsidiarity: A preliminary discussion paper', Paper presented to the Lisbon International Symposium on Global Drug Policy, 23–24 October, Lisbon

Bromley, D. W. (1989) *Economic Interests and Institutions: The Conceptual Foundations of Public Policy*, Basil Blackwell, New York

Bromley, D. W. (2004) 'Reconsidering environmental policy: Prescriptive consequentialism and volitional pragmatism', *Environmental and Resource Economics*, vol 28, pp73–99

Bromley, R., and Bustelo, E. (1982) 'Introduction', in Bromley, R. and Bustelo, E. (eds) *Politica y Technica No Planajamento: Prospectivas Criticas*, United Nations Children's Fund, Brasilia, pp9–11

Bromley, D. W., and Cernea, M. M. (1989) *The Management of Common Property Natural Resources: Some Conceptual and Operational Fallacies*, World Bank, Washington, DC

Bryan, T. A. (2004) 'Tragedy averted: The promise of collaboration', *Society and Natural Resources*, vol 17, pp881–896

Buchanan, J. M. (1954) 'Social choice, democracy, and free markets', *Journal of Political Economy*, vol 62, pp114–123

Buchanan, J. M., and Tulloch, G. (1962) *The Calculus of Consent: The Logical Foundations of Constitutional Democracy*, University of Michigan Press, Ann Arbor

Camazine, S., Deneubourg, J. L., Franks, N. R., Sney, J., Theraulaz, G., and Bonabeau, E. (2001) *Self-organization in Biological Systems*, Princeton University Press, Princeton

Carozza, P. G. (2003) 'Subsidiarity as a structural principle of international human rights law', *American Journal of International Law*, vol 97, pp38–79

Challen, R. (2000) *Institutions, Transaction Costs and Environmental Policy: Institutional Reform for Water Resources*, Edward Elgar, Cheltenham

Child, B. (2003) 'Origins and efficacy of modern CBNRM Practices in the Southern African Region', in Whande, W., Kepe, T. and Murphree, M. (eds) *Local Communities, Equity and Conservation in Southern Africa*, Programme for Land and Agrarian Studies, University of Western Cape, Cape Town, pp33–39

Child, B. and Clayton, B. D. (2004) 'Transforming approaches to CBNRM: Learning from the Luangwa Experience in Zambia', in McShane, T. O. and Wells, M. P. (eds) *Getting Biodiversity Projects to Work: Towards More Effective Conservation and Development*, Columbia University Press, New York

Chong, D. (1991) *Collective Action and the Civil Rights Movement*, University of Chicago Press, Chicago

Ciriacy-Wantrup, S. V. (1971) 'The economics of environmental policy', *Land Economics*, vol 47, pp36–45

Coase, R. H. (1937) 'The nature of the firm', *Economica*, vol 4, pp386–405

Coase, R. H. (1960) 'The problem of social cost', *Journal of Law and Economics*, vol 3, pp1–44

Cohen, J. (1998) 'Democracy and liberty', in Elster, J. (ed) *Deliberative Democracy*, Cambridge University Press, Cambridge, pp185–231

Colander, D. (2000a) 'New millennium economics: How did it get this way, and what way is it?', *Journal of Economic Perspectives*, vol 14, pp121–132

Colander, D. (2000b) 'A thumbnail sketch of the history of thought from a complexity perspective', in Colander, D. (ed.) *Complexity and the History of Economic Thought: Perspectives on the History of Economic Thought*, Routledge, London and New York, pp31–43

Conley, A., and Moote, M. (2003) 'Evaluating collaborative natural resource management', *Society and Natural Resources*, vol 16, pp371–386

Connor, R., and Dovers, S. (2004) *Institutional Change for Sustainable Development*, Edward Elgar Publishing, Cheltenham

Cosmides, L., and Tooby, J. (1992) 'Cognitive adaptations for social exchange', in Barkow, J. H., Cosmides, L. and Tooby, J. (eds) *The Adapted Mind: Evolutionary Psychology and the Generation of Culture*, Oxford University Press, New York, pp163–228

Croly, H. (1909) *The Promise of American Life*, Macmillan, New York

David, P. A. (1985) 'Clio and the economics of QWERTY', *American Economic Review*, vol 75, pp332–337

Dawes, R., van de Kragt, A. J. C., and Orbell, J. M. (1990) 'Cooperation for the benefit of us? Not me, or my conscience', in Mansbridge, J. (ed.) *Beyond Self Interest*, University of Chicago Press, Chicago

Day, G. (1998) 'Working with the grain? Towards sustainable rural and community development', *Journal of Rural Studies*, vol 14, pp89–105

de Sousa, R. (1987) *The Rationality of Emotion*, MIT Press, Cambridge, MA

deGrassi, A. (2003) *Constructing subsidiarity, consolidating hegemony: Political economy and agro-ecological processes in Ghanaian forestry*, Environmental Governance in Africa Working Paper 13, World Resources Institute, Washington, DC

Demsetz, H. (1967) 'Toward a theory of property rights', *American Economic Review*, vol 57, pp347–359

Demsetz, H. (1969) 'Information and efficiency: Another viewpoint', *Journal of Law and Economics*, vol 12, pp1–22

Denzau, A. T. and North, D. C. (1994) 'Shared mental models: Ideologies and institutions', *Kyklos*, vol 47, pp3–32

Dixit, A. K. (1996) *The Making of Economic Policy: A Transaction-Cost Politics Perspective*, MIT Press, Cambridge, MA

Dovers, S. (1999a) 'Antidotes and correctives to *ad hocery* and amnesia: Some thoughts for the Murray-Darling basin policy community', Paper commissioned by the Murray-Darling Basin Commission, Centre for Resource and Environmental Studies, Canberra

Dovers, S. (1999b) 'Public policy and institutional R&D for natural resource management: Issues and directions for LWRRDC', in Mobbs, C. and Dovers, S. (eds) *Social, Economic, Legal, Policy and Institutional R&D for Natural Resource Management: Issues and Directions for LWRRDC*, Land and Water Resources Research and Development Corporation, Canberra, pp78–107

Easterby-Smith, M., Thorpe, R. and Lowe, A. (1991) *Management Research: An Introduction*, Sage, London

Edwards, V. M. and Steins, N. A. (1998) 'Developing an analytical framework for multiple-use commons', *Journal of Theoretical Politics*, vol 10, pp347–383

Ellickson, R. C. (1991) *Order Without Law: How Neighbors Settle Disputes*, Harvard University Press, Cambridge, MA

Elster, J. (1998) 'Emotions and economic theory', *Journal of Economic Literature*, vol 36, pp47–74

Ezrahi, Y. (1990) *The Descent of Icarus: Science and the Transformation of Contemporary Democracy*, Harvard University Press, Cambridge, MA

Fairbanks, M. (2000) 'Changing the mind of a nation: Elements in a process for creating prosperity', in Harrison, L. E. and Huntington, S. P. (eds) *Culture Matters: How Values Shape Human Progress*, Basic Books, New York, pp268–281

Frank, R. H. (1990) 'A theory of moral sentiments', in Mansbridge, J. J. (ed.) *Beyond Self-Interest*, University of Chicago Press, Chicago, pp71–96

Frey, B. S. and Eichenberger, R. (1999) *The New Democratic Federalism for Europe: Functional, Overlapping and Competing Jurisdictions*, Edward Elgar Publishing, Cheltenham

Friedman, M. (1953) *Essays in Positive Economics*, Chicago University Press, Chicago

Gächter, S., and Fehr, E. (1999) 'Collective action as a social exchange', *Journal of Economic Behavior and Organization*, vol 39, pp341–369

Gordon, H. S. (1954) 'The economic theory of a common property resource: The fishery', *The Journal of Political Economy*, vol 62, pp124–142

Granovetter, M. (1973) 'The strength of weak ties', *American Journal of Sociology*, vol 78, pp1360–1380

Gray, B. (1985) 'Conditions facilitating interorganizational collaboration', *Human Relations*, vol 38, pp911–936

Hajkowicz, S., Young, M., Wheeler, S., McDonald, D. H. and Young, D. (2000) *Supporting decisions: Understanding natural resource management techniques*, Policy and Economic Research Unit, CSIRO Land and Water, Adelaide, www.lwa.gov.au/downloads/publications_pdf/PF010171.pdf

Hardin, G. (1968) 'The tragedy of the commons', *Science*, vol 162, pp1243–1248

Hardin, R. (1971) 'Collective action as an agreeable n-prisoner's dilemma', *Behavioral Science*, vol 16, pp472–481

Hardin, R. (1982) *Collective Action*, John Hopkins Press, Baltimore

Hardin, R. (1993) 'The street-level epistemology of trust', *Politics and Society*, vol 21, pp505–529

Harrison, L. E. (1997) *The Pan-American Dream*, Basic Books, New York

Hartig, J. H., Law, N. L., Epstein, D., Fuller, K., Letterhos, J. and Krantzberg, G. (1995) 'Capacity building for restoring degraded areas in the Great Lakes', *International Journal of Sustainable Development and World Ecology*, vol 2, pp1–10

Hayek, F. A. (1945) 'The use of knowledge in society', *American Economic Review*, vol 35, pp519–520

Hays, S. P. (1959) *Conservation and the Gospel of Efficiency: The Progressive Conservation Movement 1890–1920*, Harvard University Press, Cambridge, MA

Hermalin, B. E. (1998) 'Toward an economic theory of leadership', *American Economic Review*, vol 88, pp1188–1206

Holling, C. S. (2004) 'From complex regions to complex worlds', *Ecology and Society* vol 9, p11, www.ecologyandsociety.org/vol9/iss1/art11

Hussey, J. and Hussey, R. (1997) *Business Research: A Practical Guide for Undergraduate and Postgraduate Students*, Macmillan Business, Houndmills

Huxham, C. and Vangen, S. (2000a) 'Leadership in the shaping and implementation of collaboration agendas: How things happen in a (not quite) joined-up world', *Academy of Management Journal*, vol 43, pp1159–1175

Huxham, C. and Vangen, S. (2000b) 'What makes partnerships work?', in Osbourne, S. P. (ed.) *Public–Private Partnerships*, Routledge, London and New York, pp293–310

Innes, J. E. and Booher, D. E. (2003) 'Collaborative policy-making: Governance through dialogue', in Hajer, M. A. and Wagenaar, H. (eds) *Deliberative Policy Analysis: Understanding Governance in the Network Society*, Cambridge University Press, Cambridge, pp33–59

International Union for the Conservation of Nature (1980) *World Conservation Strategy*, International Union for the Conservation of Nature, Gland

Jacobs, J. (1992[1961]) *The Death and Life of Great American Cities*, Vintage Books, New York

Jiggins, J. and Röling, N. (2002) 'Adaptive management: Potential and limitations for ecological governance', *International Journal of Agricultural Resources, Governance and Ecology*, vol 1, pp28–42

Kiser, L. L. and Ostrom, E. (1982) 'The three worlds of action: A metatheoretical synthesis of institutional approaches', in Ostrom, E. (ed.) *Strategies of Political Inquiry*, Sage Publications, Beverly Hills, pp179–222

Knight, F. (1947) *Freedom and Reform: Essays in Economic and Social Philosophy*, Harper, New York

Knox, A. and Meinzen-Dick, R. (2001) *Collective action, property rights, and devolution of natural resource management: Exchange of knowledge and implications for policy*, CAPRi Working Paper No. 11, CGIAR Systemwide Program on Collective Action and Property Rights, Washington, DC

Koontz, T. M., Steelman, T. A., Carmin, J., Korfmacher, K. S., Mosely, C. and Thomas, C. W. (2004) *Collaborative Environmental Management: What Roles for Government?*, Resources for the Future, Washington, DC

Kotter, J. P. (1995) 'Leading change: Why transformation efforts fail', *Harvard Business Review*, March–April, pp59–67

Krishna, A. (1997) 'Participatory watershed development and soil conservation in Rajasthan, India', in Krishna, A., Uphoff, N. and Esman, M. J. (eds) *Reasons for Hope: Instructive Experiences in Rural Development*, Kumarian Press, West Hartford, pp255–272

Kuhn, T. (1970) *The Structure of Scientific Revolutions*, 2nd edition, University of Chicago Press, Chicago

Lane, M. B. (2003) 'Decentralization or privatization of environmental governance? Forest conflict and bioregional assessment in Australia', *Journal of Rural Studies*, vol 19, pp283–294

Lecomte, B. J. and Krishna, A. (1997) 'Six-S: Building on traditional social organizations', in Krishna, A., Uphoff, N. and Esman, M. J. (eds) *Reasons for Hope: Instructive Experiences in Rural Development*, Kumarian Press, West Hartford, pp75–90

Lichbach, M. I. (1996) *The Cooperator's Dilemma*, University of Michigan Press, Ann Arbor

Lindblom, C. E. (1965) *The Intelligence of Democracy: Decision Making through Mutual Adjustment*, Free Press, New York

Lindsay, S. (2000) 'Culture, mental models, and national prosperity', in Harrison, L. E. and Huntington, S. P. (eds) *Culture Matters: How Values Shape Human Progress*, Basic Books, New York, pp282–295

Mandondo, A. (2000), *Situating Zimbabwe's natural resource governance systems in history*, Occasional Paper No. 32, Center for International Forestry Research, Bogor, Indonesia

Mansuri, G. and Rao, V. (2003) *Evaluating Community-based and Community-driven Development: A Critical Review of the Evidence*, Development Research Group, World Bank, Washington, DC

March, J. G. and Simon, H. A. (1958) *Organizations*, John Wiley and Sons, New York

Margerum, R. D. (1999) 'Getting past yes: From capital creation to action', *Journal of the American Planning Association*, vol 65, pp181–192

Marshall, A. (1920[1890]) *Principles of Economics: An Introductory Volume*, 8th edition, Macmillan, London

Marshall, G. R. (2004a) 'Farmers cooperating in the commons? A study of collective action in salinity management', *Ecological Economics* vol 51, pp271–286

Marshall, G. R. (2004b) 'From words to deeds: Enforcing farmers' conservation cost-sharing commitments', *Journal of Rural Studies*, vol 20, pp157–167

McCann, L., Colby, B., Easter, K. W., Kasterine, A. and Kuperan, K. V. (in press) 'Transaction cost measurement for evaluating environmental policies', *Ecological Economics*[Q5]

McKean, M. A. (2002) 'Nesting institutions for complex common-pool resource systems', in Graham, J., Reeve, I. and Brunckhorst, D. (eds) *Landscape Futures II: Social and Institutional Dimensions. Proceedings of the 2nd International Symposium on Landscape Futures, Armidale, 4–6 December 2001*, Institute for Rural Futures, University of New England, Armidale

Meadows, D. H., Meadows, D. L., Randers, J. and Behrens III, W. (1972) *The Limits to Growth*, Universe Books, New York

Meinzen-Dick, R., Di Gregorio, M. and McCarthy, N. (2004) *Methods for studying collective action in rural development*, CAPRi Working Paper No 33, CGIAR Systemwide Program on Collective Action and Property Rights, Washington, DC

Metcalfe, S. (1997) 'The CAMPFIRE Program: Community-based wildlife resource management in Zimbabwe', in Krishna, A., Uphoff, N. and Esman, M. J. (eds) *Reasons for Hope: Instructive Experiences in Rural Development*, Kumarian Press, West Hartford, pp273–288

Mitchell, W. C. (1945) 'The National Bureau's first quarter-century', *25th Annual Report*, National Bureau of Economic Research, Washington, DC

Mobbs, C. and Dovers, S. (eds) (1999) *Social, Economic, Legal, Policy and Institutional R&D for Natural Resource Management: Issues and Directions for LWRRDC*, Occasional Paper No. 01/99, Land and Water Resources Research and Development Corporation, Canberra

Moore, E. A. and Koontz, T. M. (2003) 'A typology of collaborative watershed groups: Citizen-based, agency-based, and mixed partnerships', *Society and Natural*

Resources, vol 16, pp451–460

Murray Darling Basin Commission (undated) *Online basin encyclopedia,* Murray Darling Basin Commission website, www.mdbc.gov.au/education/education.htm

Murray Irrigation Limited (1998) *1997–98 Environment Report Summary,* Murray Irrigation Limited, Deniliquin

Nash, J. (1951) 'Non-cooperative games', *Annals of Mathematics,* vol 54, pp286–295

Nee, V. (1998) 'Norms and networks in economic and organizational performance', *American Economic Review,* vol 88, pp85–89

Neimark, P. and Mott, P. R. (eds) (1999) *The Environmental Debate: A Documentary History,* Greenwood Press, Westport

Nelson, R. H. (1987) 'The economics profession and the making of public policy', *Journal of Economic Literature,* vol 25, pp49–91

Norgaard, R. B. (1994) *Development Betrayed: The End of Progress and a Coevolutionary Revisioning of the Future,* Routledge, London

Norris, P. (1999a) 'Conclusions: The growth of critical citizens and its consequences', in Norris, P. (ed.) *Critical Citizens: Global Support for Democratic Governance,* Oxford University Press, New York, pp257–272

Norris, P. (1999b) 'Introduction: The growth of critical citizens?', in Norris, P. (ed.) *Critical Citizens: Global Support for Democratic Governance,* Oxford University Press, New York, pp1–27

North, D. C. (1990) *Institutions, Institutional Change and Economic Performance,* Cambridge University Press, Cambridge

North, D. C. (1994) 'Economic performance through time', *American Economic Review,* vol 84, pp359–369

North, D. C. (2005) *Understanding the Process of Economic Change,* Princeton University Press, Princeton.

Norton, B., Costanza, R. and Bishop, R. C. (1998) 'The evolution of preferences: Why "sovereign" preferences may not lead to sustainable policies and what to do about it', *Ecological Economics,* vol 24, pp193–211

Oakerson, R. J. (1986) 'A model for the analysis of common property problems', in *Proceedings of the Conference on Common Property Resource Management,* National Academy Press, Washington, DC, pp13–20

Oakerson, R. J. (1992) 'Analyzing the commons: A framework', in Bromley, D. W. (ed.) *Making the Commons Work: Theory, Practice, and Policy,* ICS Press, San Francisco, pp41–59

O'Connor, M. (2000), *Our common problems: ICT, the Prisoners' Dilemma, and the process of working out reasonable solutions to impossible environmental problems,* Cahier no. 00-06, Centre d'Economie et d'Ethique pour l'Environnement et le Development, Université de Versailles St-Quentin-en-Yvelines, Guyancourt

Olson, M. (1965) *The Logic of Collective Action,* Harvard University Press, Cambridge, MA

Ostrom, E. (1990) *Governing the Commons: The Evolution of Institutions for Collective Action,* Cambridge University Press, Cambridge

Ostrom, E. (1998a) 'A behavioral approach to the rational choice theory of collective action, *American Political Science Review,* vol 92, pp1–22

Ostrom, E. (1998b) 'The Institutional Analysis and Development approach', in Loehman, E. T. and Kilgour, D. M. (eds) *Designing Institutions for Environmental and Resource Management,* Edward Elgar, Cheltenham, pp68–90

Ostrom, E. (1999) 'Coping with tragedies of the commons', *Annual Review of Political Science,* vol 2, pp493–535

Ostrom, E. (2000a) 'Collective action and the evolution of social norms', *Journal of Economic Perspectives,* vol 14, pp137–158

Ostrom, E. (2000b) *Decentralization and development: The new panacea,* Working Paper No. W00-4, Workshop in Political Theory and Policy Analysis, Indiana

University, Bloomington

Ostrom, E., (2005) *Understanding Institutional Diversity*, Princeton University Press, Princeton.

Ostrom, E., Gardner, R. and Walker, J. (1994a) 'Regularities from the laboratory and possible explanations', in Ostrom, E., Gardner, R. and Walker, J. (eds) *Rules, Games, and Common-Pool Resources*, University of Michigan Press, Ann Arbor, pp195–220

Ostrom, E., Gardner, R. and Walker, J. (eds) (1994b) *Rules, Games and Common-Pool Resources*, University of Michigan Press, Ann Arbor

Ostrom, E., Burger, J., Field, C. B., Norgaard, R. B. and Policansky, D. (1999a) 'Revisiting the commons: Local lessons, global challenges', *Science*, vol 284, pp278–282

Ostrom, V., Tiebout, C. M. and Warren, R. (1999b[1961]) 'The organization of government in metropolitan areas: A theoretical inquiry', in McGinnis, M. D. (ed.) *Polycentricity and Local Public Economies: Readings from the Workshop in Political Theory and Policy Analysis*, University of Michigan Press, Ann Arbor, pp31–51

Owens, S. (2000) '"Engaging the public": Information and deliberation in environmental policy', *Environment and Planning A*, vol 32, pp1141–1148

Pearce, D., Markandya, A. and Barbier, E. D. (1989) *Blueprint for a Green Economy*. Earthscan Publications, London

Pezzey, J. C. V. and Toman, M. A. (2002) 'Introduction', in Pezzey, J. C. V. and Toman, M. A. (eds) *The Economics of Sustainability*, Ashgate Publishing, Dartmouth, ppxi–xxxii

Porter, T. M. (1995) *Trust in Numbers: The Pursuit of Objectivity in Science and Public Life*, Princeton University Press, Princeton

Posner, R. A. (1997) 'Social norms and the law: An economic approach', *American Economic Review*, vol 87, pp365–369

Posner, R. A. and Rasmussen, E. B. (1999) 'Creating and enforcing norms, with special reference to sanctions', *International Review of Law and Economics*, vol 19, pp369–382

Poteete, A. and Ostrom, E. (2003) *In pursuit of comparable concepts and data about collective action*, CAPRi Working Paper No. 29, CGIAR Systemwide Program on Collective Action and Property Rights, Washington, DC

Pretty, J. and Ward, H. (2001) 'Social capital and the environment', *World Development*, vol 29, pp209–227

Putnam, R. D. (1993) *Making Democracy Work: Civic Traditions in Modern Italy*, Princeton University Press, Princeton

Randall, A. (1981) *Resource Economics: An Economic Approach to Natural Resource and Environmental Policy*, Grid Publishing, Columbus

Randall, A. (1999) 'A new look at the old problem of externalities', *Choices*, First Quarter, pp29–32

Rhoades, R. E. (2000) 'The participatory multipurpose watershed project: Nature's salvation or Schumacher's nightmare?', in Lal, R. (ed.) *Integrated Watershed Management in the Global Ecosystem*, CRC Press, Boca Raton, pp327–343

Ribot, J. C. (2002) *Democratic Decentralization of Natural Resources: Institutionalizing Popular Participation*, World Resources Institute, Washington, DC

Robinson, M. (1996) 'Constitutional shifts in Europe and the US: Learning from each other', *Stanford Journal of International Law*, vol 32, pp1–12

Rudd, M. (2004) 'An institutional framework for designing and monitoring ecosystem-based fisheries management policy experiments', *Ecological Economics*, vol 48, pp109–124

Runge, C. F. (1981) 'Common property externalities: Isolation, assurance, and resource depletion in a traditional grazing context', *American Journal of Agricultural Economics*, vol 63, pp595–605

Sally, D. (1995) 'Conservation and cooperation in social dilemmas: A meta-analysis of experiments from 1958 to 1992', *Rationality and Society*, vol 7, pp58–92

Schlager, E. and Ostrom, E. (1992) 'Property-rights regimes and natural resources: A conceptual analysis', *Land Economics*, vol 68, pp249–262

Schmid, A. A. (1989) *Benefit–cost Analysis: A Political Economy Approach*, Westview Press, Boulder

Schmid, A. A. (2004) *Conflict and Cooperation: Institutional and Behavioral Economics*, Blackwell Publishing, Malden

Schroo, H. (1998) 'Licensing of privatised and corporatised irrigation schemes in NSW', Paper presented to the ANCID 1998 Conference 'Living with Limited Water', August, at Sale, Victoria

Schumacher, E. F. (1973) *Small is Beautiful: A Study of Economics as if People Mattered*, Blond and Briggs, London

Scott, A. D. (1955) 'The fishery: The objectives of sole ownership', *Journal of Political Economy*, vol 63, pp116–124

Selin, S. and Chavez, D. (1995) 'Developing a collaborative model for environmental planning and management', *Environmental Management*, vol 19, pp189–195

Sen, A. K. (1995) 'Rationality and social choice', *American Economic Review*, vol 85, pp1–24

Senge, P. M. (1990) *The Fifth Discipline: The Art and Practice of the Learning Organization*, Random House, Sydney

Simon, H. A. (1946) 'The proverbs of administration', *Public Administration Review*, vol 6, pp53–67

Simon, H. A. (1955) 'A behavioral model of rational choice', *Quarterly Journal of Economics*, vol 69, pp99–118

Slater, G. and Spencer, D. A. (2000) 'The uncertain foundations of transaction cost economics', *Journal of Economic Issues*, vol 34, pp61–87

Sproule-Jones, M. (2002) *Restoration of the Great Lakes: Promises, Practices, Performances*, UBC Press, Vancouver

Stevenson, G. G. (1991) *Common Property Economics: A General Theory and Land Use Applications*, Cambridge University Press, Cambridge

Stretton, H. and Orchard, L. (1994) *Public Goods, Public Enterprise, Public Choice: Theoretical Foundations of the Contemporary Attack on Government*, St Martin's Press, New York

Sugden, R. (1986) *The Economics of Rights, Co-operation and Welfare*, Blackwell, Oxford

Thompson, D. B. (1999) 'Beyond benefit–cost analysis: Institutional transaction costs and regulation of water quality', *Natural Resources Journal*, vol 39, pp517–541

United Nations (1992a) *Agenda 21*, United Nations, New York

United Nations (1992b) *Rio Declaration on Environment and Development*, Annex 1 in the Report of the United Nations Conference on Environment and Development, United Nations, New York

United Nations (2002) *Report of the World Summit on Sustainable World Development, Johannesburg, South Africa*, United Nations, New York

United Nations Environment Programme (2002) *Global Environment Outlook 3: Past, Present and Future Perspectives*, Earthscan Publications, London

Uphoff, N., Esman, M. J. and Krishna, A. (1998) *Reasons for Success: Learning from Instructive Experiences in Rural Development*, Kumarian Press, West Hartford

Wacquant, L. J. D. (1993) 'Positivism', in Outhwaite, W. and Bottomore, T. (eds) *The Blackwell Dictionary of Twentieth-Century Social Thought*, Blackwell, Oxford, pp495–498

Wallis, J. and Dollery, B. (1995) 'A communitarian perspective on government failure, *International Journal of Social Economics*, vol 22, pp33–48

Wallis, J. and Dollery, B. (1999) *Market Failure, Government Failure, Leadership and*

Public Policy, Macmillan Press, Houndmills

Walters, C. J. (1986) *Adaptive Management of Renewable Resources*, Macmillan, New York

Wells, D. and Lynch, T. (2000) *The Political Ecologist*, Ashgate, Aldershot

Wijayaratna, C. M. and Uphoff, N. (1997) 'Farmer organization in Gal Oya: Improving irrigation management in Sri Lanka', in Krishna, A., Uphoff, N. and Esman, M. J. (eds) *Reasons for Hope: Instructive Experiences in Rural Development*, Kumarian Press, West Hartford, pp166–183

Williamson, O. E. (1975) *Markets and Hierarchies: Analysis and Antitrust Implications*, Free Press, New York

Williamson, O. E. (1985) *The Economic Institutions of Capitalism*, Free Press, New York

Williamson, O. E. (1996) *The Mechanisms of Governance*, Oxford University Press, New York, USA

Williamson, O. E. (2000) 'The new institutional economics: Taking stock, looking ahead', *Journal of Economic Literature*, vol 38, pp595–613

Wilson, E. O. (1999) *Consilience: The Unity of Knowledge*, Abacus, London

Wilson, J. (2002) 'Scientific uncertainty, complex systems, and the design of common-pool institutions', in Ostrom, E., Dietz, T., Dolšak, N., Stern, P. C., Stonich, S. and Weber, E. U. (eds) *The Drama of the Commons*, National Academy Press, Washington, DC, pp327–359

Wondolleck, J. M. and Yaffee, S. L. (2000) *Making Collaboration Work: Lessons from Innovation in Natural Resource Management*, Island Press, Washington, DC

World Bank (1993) *Water Resources Management: A World Bank Policy Paper*, Washington, DC

World Commission on Environment and Development (1987) *Our Common Future*, Oxford University Press, Oxford

Yin, R. K. (1984) *Case Study Research*, Sage Publications, Beverly Hills

Young, O. R. (2002a) *The Institutional Dimensions of Environmental Change: Fit, Interplay, and Scale*, MIT Press, Cambridge, MA

Young, O. R. (2002b) 'Institutional interplay: The environmental consequences of cross-scale interactions', in Ostrom, E., Dietz, T., Dolšak, N., Stern, P. C., Stonich, S. and Weber, E. U. (eds) *The Drama of the Commons*, National Academy Press, Washington, DC, pp263–291

Index